A STRATEGY FOR
IMF REFORM

A STRATEGY FOR IMF REFORM

Edwin M. Truman

INSTITUTE FOR INTERNATIONAL ECONOMICS
Washington, DC
February 2006

Edwin M. Truman, senior fellow since 2001, was assistant secretary of the Treasury for international affairs (1998–2000). He directed the Division of International Finance of the Board of Governors of the Federal Reserve System from 1977 to 1998. From 1983 to 1998, he was one of three economists on the staff of the Federal Open Market Committee. He has been a member of numerous international economic and financial issues. He is the author of *Inflation Targeting in the World Economy* (2003) and coauthor of *Chasing Dirty Money: The Fight Against Money Laundering* (2004).

**INSTITUTE FOR
INTERNATIONAL ECONOMICS**
1750 Massachusetts Avenue, NW
Washington, DC 20036-1903
(202) 328-9000   FAX: (202) 659-3225
www.iie.com

C. Fred Bergsten, *Director*
Valerie Norville, *Director of Publications
    and Web Development*
Edward Tureen, *Director of Marketing*

Typesetting by BMWW
Printing by United Book Press, Inc.

For reprints/permission to photocopy please contact the APS customer service department at Copyright Clearance Center, Inc., 222 Rosewood Drive, Danvers, MA 01923; or email requests to:
info@copyright.com

Printed in the United States of America

08 07 06   5 4 3 2 1

Library of Congress Cataloging-in-Publication Data

Truman, Edwin M.
    A strategy for IMF reform / Edwin M. Truman.
        p. cm.—(Policy analyses in international economics; 77)
    Includes bibliographical references and index.
        ISBN 0-88132-398-5 (alk. paper)/
            978-0-88132-398-6
    1. International Monetary Fund.
2. International finance. I. Title: strategy for International Monetary Fund reform.
II. Title. III. Series.

HG3881.5.I58.T74 2006
332.1'52—dc22

                            2005036413

Contents

Preface   **vii**

Author's Note   **xi**

1 The Agenda for IMF Reform   **1**
The Case for IMF Reform   2
The Content of IMF Reform   4
An IMF Reform Package   6
Final Comments   20

2 IMF Activities and Reform Efforts   **23**
Mandate   23
Tools and Activities   28
Facts about the IMF and Its Lending   31
IMF Reform Efforts   39

3 Role in the International Monetary System   **45**
Surveillance   46
Exchange Rates and Policies   50
Capital Accounts and Financial Sectors   52
Regional Arrangements   56

4 Governance   **61**
Quotas and Voting Power   64
Choice of Management and Staff   71

Chairs and Reform of the Executive Board   73
The IMF and Steering Committees   77

5 **Lending Facilities**   **83**
   The IMF as an International Lender   90
   Support for Members with Large Debts   97
   IMF Lending Programs for Good Performers   98
   Support Without Lending   100
   Support for Low-Income Countries   102

6 **Financial Resources**   **107**
   The IMF's Need for More Resources   108
   Augmenting the IMF's Resources   110
   The Future of SDR   113

References   **117**

Index   **125**

Tables

Table 2.1 IMF members, 2005   32
Table 2.2 Composition of IMF membership, 2005 and 1975   33
Table 2.3 Distribution of members with IMF credit outstanding,
           1975–2005   34
Table 2.4 Distribution of IMF credit outstanding, 1975–2005 35
Table 2.5 Proportion of countries within groups with credit
           outstanding, 1975–2005   36
Table 5.1 Countries borrowing from the IMF, 1970–2005   85
Table 6.1 IMF quotas relative to reserves, GDP, and trade 109

Boxes

Box 1.1 Managing Director de Rato's Report on the Fund's
         Medium-Term Strategy   2
Box 1.2 Michel Camdessus's reform agenda   7

Preface

The role of the International Monetary Fund (IMF) has been a constant focus of the research program of the Institute for International Economics since its inception in 1981. The Institute's initial publications were in fact *The Lending Policies of the International Monetary Fund*, and the conference volume *IMF Conditionality* from which it was drawn, both authored by Senior Fellow John Williamson.

This priority attention reflects both the central responsibilities of the Fund for the effective functioning of the international monetary system and continuing widespread dissatisfaction with its ability to adapt sufficiently to the changing needs of the system. The consequent calls for reform of "the international financial architecture," notably including the policies and operations of the Fund, reached new heights with the financial crises of the 1990s (Mexico, East Asia, Russia, Brazil, and subsequently Argentina) and the sharp attacks, which continue to this day, on its alleged failures to either prevent those disruptions or respond effectively to them.

This new study attempts to present a comprehensive overview of the challenges facing the IMF in the early years of the 21st century and what new reforms are needed to enable it to provide the needed leadership of the international monetary system. Recognizing that some changes have already been made, author Edwin M. Truman concludes that the Fund nevertheless needs to adopt substantial further modifications to restore its essential role at the center of the system. Eschewing the generalizations that sometimes characterize the debate on this topic, Truman offers a series of very specific proposals through which the IMF can reform its own governance structure, which he regards as a necessary precondition for successfully conducting all the other needed improvements; restore its central position in fostering constructive global adjustment, including by the rich industrial economies and through a much more active role in guiding the exchange rate system; sharply improve its ability to prevent crises, especially in emerging-market economies; and respond more effectively to those crises that, whatever other reforms are undertaken, will inevitably occur (especially in those emerging markets) from time to time.

This study is drawn from the larger publication *Reforming the IMF for the 21st Century*, which the Institute will publish shortly and which presents the papers presented to the conference we held on IMF reform on September 23, 2005. Those papers offer a wide range of analyses of the problems facing the Fund and a rich menu of possible improvements in its functioning. Truman organized the conference and prepared both the overview background paper on which it was based, included in this policy analysis, and the chapter that summarizes its main findings and proposals. This shorter publication, which is intended to reach a broader audience that may not wish to peruse all the contributions to the conference, draws heavily on those papers but represents his personal views on the challenges facing the Fund and the needed reform agenda.

Truman is uniquely qualified to offer these proposals. He served from 1977 to 1998 as director of the Division of International Finance of the Board of Governors of the Federal Reserve System, and thus as the chief adviser to Chairmen Paul A. Volcker and Alan Greenspan on the entire range of international financial problems (including crises) that marked that turbulent period. He then became assistant secretary of the Treasury for international affairs during 1998–2001, playing a key role as a member of the "Committee to Save the World" (as it was called by *Time*) during the crises of that period. He thus brings to this project enormous personal experience with the IMF as well as the keen analytical talents of a top economist who has published two major books, *Chasing Dirty Money: The Fight Against Money Laundering* and *Inflation Targeting in the World Economy*, since becoming a senior fellow at the Institute in 2001.

The Institute for International Economics is a private, nonprofit institution for the study and discussion of international economic policy. Its purpose is to analyze important issues in that area and to develop and communicate practical new approaches for dealing with them. The Institute is completely nonpartisan.

The Institute is funded by a highly diversified group of philanthropic foundations, private corporations, and interested individuals. Major institutional grants are now being received from the William M. Keck, Jr. Foundation and the Starr Foundation. About 33 percent of the Institute's resources in our latest fiscal year were provided by contributors outside the United States, including about 16 percent from Japan. The Rockefeller Brothers Fund supported the very important component of this project devoted to improving the governance of the IMF, especially to provide a greater voice for developing countries.

The Institute's Board of Directors bears overall responsibilities for the Institute and gives general guidance and approval to its research program, including the identification of topics that are likely to become important over the medium run (one to three years) and that should be addressed by the Institute. The director, working closely with the staff and outside Advisory Committee, is responsible for the development of particular projects and makes the final decision to publish an individual study.

The Institute hopes that its studies and other activities will contribute to building a stronger foundation for international economic policy around the world. We invite readers of these publications to let us know how they think we can best accomplish this objective.

C. FRED BERGSTEN
Director
December 2005

Author's Note

The International Monetary Fund (IMF) is a major pillar of the post–World War II international architecture that has facilitated unprecedented economic expansion for most, though not all, participants in the global economy. Today, the IMF is under stress. It risks declining into irrelevance or becoming primarily one more institution, among the many, assisting the poorest countries. To restore the IMF to its central role, it must be reformed. Unfortunately, there is no consensus on the appropriate direction and content of such reform.

This policy analysis and the associated conference at the Institute for International Economics in September 2005 are intended to help shape a consensus on IMF reform. Chapter 1 presents my IMF reform agenda. No one is expected to endorse all of its elements; my aim is to sketch out a balanced package. The subsequent chapters provide background analysis: Chapter 2 describes the IMF's activities and previous reforms. Chapter 3 addresses the IMF's role in the evolving international monetary system covering surveillance, exchange rate regimes, capital accounts and financial sectors, and the IMF's relations with regional arrangements. Chapter 4 considers the central issues of IMF governance: the distribution of IMF quotas and voting power, the choice of the institution's management and staff, reform of the IMF Executive Board, and the institution's relationship with various actual and potential steering committees for the world economic system. Chapter 5 takes up the topic of IMF lending activities, including the Fund's support for members with large debts, its programs for countries that have good records of economic performance, and its engagement with low-income members. Chapter 6 concludes by reviewing the adequacy of the IMF's financial resources, how best to augment those resources when and if there is a need, and the future of special drawing rights issued by the IMF.

This policy analysis, the associated conference, and the subsequent conference volume could not have been completed without the support and guidance of many people. The Institute's Director C. Fred Bergsten shared the same broad concerns that motivated me to undertake this project. Without his active participation and constant support, the results would have been substantially inferior. Anna Wong provided admirable research and other assistance on all aspects of the project. I am also very grateful to the participants in the conference whose papers and comments have helped to shape my thinking.

I am indebted for comments on the content of earlier versions of what appears in chapters 2 to 6 of this policy analysis to Lewis Alexander, C. Fred Bergsten, Jack Boorman, James Boughton, Scott Brown, Ralph Bryant, Agustin Carstens, Tom Dawson, Timothy Geithner, Anna Gelpern, Morris Goldstein, Graham Hacche, Michael Kaplan, Anne Krueger, Tim Lane, Daniel Marx, Mike Mussa, Larry Promisel, Brad Setser, Jeff Shafer, Charles Siegman, Mark Sobel, Tracy Truman, John Williamson, and Jeromin Zettelmeyer. None of these individuals or the institutions with which they are associated is responsible for views expressed or the errors that remain.

Finally, many thanks to the skilled and patient individuals at the Institute who facilitate the transformation of written words into published volumes—Valerie Norville and her colleagues Ed Tureen, Marla Banov, and in particular Madona Devasahayam. They are terrific!

The Agenda for IMF Reform

The world needs a strong and effective International Monetary Fund (IMF) as the principal multilateral institution responsible for international economic and financial stability. A consensus on the role of the Fund and the scope of its activities in the 21st century is needed to achieve this objective. However, such a consensus does not exist today in official circles or among private observers. In the view of many observers, the Fund has failed to effectively exercise its intended role as steward of the international monetary system. Consequently the IMF, once the preeminent institution of multilateral international financial cooperation, faces an identity crisis.

No single change by itself can restore the IMF to its prior position as a highly respected international monetary institution. Effective reform of the IMF must encompass many aspects of the IMF's activities—where it should become less as well as more involved. During the past decade, a large number of changes in the international financial architecture and in the IMF's operations have been put in place. Those reforms have not been sufficient to restore the IMF's luster at the center of today's international monetary and international financial system.

Successful reform of the IMF must engage the full spectrum of its members. The IMF should not focus primarily on its low-income members and the challenges of global poverty. It should not focus exclusively on international financial crises affecting a small group of vulnerable emerging-market economies. Instead, it must be engaged with each of its members on the full range of their economic and financial policies. However, the Fund should give priority attention to the policies of the 20 to 30 systemically important countries that impact the functioning of the global economy, including the policies of its wealthiest members that remain the prin-

Box 1.1   Managing Director de Rato's Report on the Fund's Medium-Term Strategy

On September 15, 2005, the IMF released Managing Director Rodrigo de Rato's Report on the Fund's Medium-Term Strategy (IMF 2005k). The report draws on preliminary discussions held at the time of the meeting of the International Monetary and Financial Committee (IMFC) in April 2005, the work of an internal committee, as well as inputs from the IMF's Executive Board. Its self-description is a strategy paper, not a five-year plan and not a reform agenda although that term has been used to describe the document. The report views IMF reform as requiring an evolution, not a revolution, at the Fund.

The report proposes globalization as its organizing principle: "Viewing the challenges through the lens of globalization holds the potential to prioritize the elements of the Fund's well defined mandate in the macroeconomic area and to address the criticisms of limited effectiveness, focus, and preparedness to face the future." It argues that 21st century globalization involving large cross-border capital movements and abrupt shifts in comparative advantage has exposed gaps in the work of the Fund with respect to surveillance, lending facilities, and governance.

The report lays out five key tasks responding to these new global conditions:

- make surveillance more effective,
- adapt to new challenges and needs in different member countries,
- help build institutions and capacity,

(box continues next page)

cipal drivers of the world economy and, therefore, are the source of the greatest risk to global economic and financial stability.[1]

The Case for IMF Reform

Managing Director Rodrigo de Rato in his remarks to the Institute for International Economics conference on IMF reform (chapter 3 of the conference volume)[2] states that the IMF is the "central institution of global

---

1. The systemically important countries include primarily the Group of Twenty (G-20) countries: the United States, the European Union as a group, Japan, Canada, and possibly one or two other industrial countries; also Argentina, Brazil, China, Egypt, India, Indonesia, Korea, Mexico, Nigeria, Russia, Saudi Arabia, South Africa, Turkey, and possibly a few other large emerging-market countries. See also footnote 3.

2. In several places, this policy analysis cites chapters in the forthcoming conference volume, *Reforming the IMF for the 21st Century*, ed. Edwin M. Truman (2006, Institute for International Economics).

2   A STRATEGY FOR IMF REFORM

Box 1.1   *(continued)*

■ prioritize and reorganize IMF work within a prudent medium-term budget, and

■ address the governance issue of fair quotas and voice (representation) in the Fund.

Against this background, the report discusses nine issues and proposes 31 actions or "deliverables" as next steps in the strategic review of the Fund by IMF management, the Executive Board, and member countries. Most proposed actions are process oriented, a few involve reoriented research efforts, and a larger number concern internal organization and management.

The report highlights four new proposals: intensified analysis of globalization, including a possible new report on the macroeconomics of globalization; a redesigned "contextually savvy" program of communication; a work program on issues surrounding capital account liberalization; and the assessment of the achievability of the Millennium Development Goals with available financing.

In keeping with the theme of a strategic review, the managing director's report suggests that these initiatives might be financed by scaling back the Fund's activities in five areas: a sharper delineation of the Fund's role in low-income countries; less time spent, in particular by the management and Executive Board, on procedures and documentation; less work on standards and codes; less research in other (unspecified) areas; and less spending on overhead and support activities, including the possibility of more offshoring of information technology services.

monetary cooperation." He suggests that the Fund can rest on its 60-year history of accomplishments, but he also acknowledges the need for changes. In fact, a few days earlier the IMF released a report by de Rato on the Fund's medium-term strategy (IMF 2005k; also box 1.1). In the report, de Rato argues that the Fund is being pulled in too many directions and accumulating new mandates: "The question [is] whether the Fund is fully prepared to meet the great macroeconomic challenges that lie ahead." On the other hand, he argues that the IMF's principal power in meeting the challenges of the 21st century is the soft power of persuasion. He implicitly dismisses proposals that the Fund should use or develop other instruments to carry out its mission. One detects little sense of urgency in his remarks.

Remarks by US Under Secretary of the Treasury for International Affairs Timothy Adams (chapter 4) convey a greater sense of potential institutional crisis than those of the IMF managing director. Adams declares he is a "believer in the IMF . . . as a facilitator of international monetary cooperation" but notes "the IMF now faces fresh, tough questions about its relevance" to the industrialized countries and to emerging-market economies. The risk is that the IMF is becoming a development institution focused primarily on its low-income members. To strengthen the Fund's relevance, Adams argues that it should concentrate on its core mission, "international financial stability and balance of payments adjustment." The IMF needs to be "far more ambitious in its surveillance of exchange rates" and by implication other macroeconomic policies. Noting that exchange rate surveillance is politically difficult, he states, "Nevertheless, the perception that the IMF is asleep at the wheel on its most fundamental responsibility—exchange rate surveillance—is very unhealthy for the institution and the international monetary system." Adams concludes that the medium-term strategy paper of the managing director represents activity but adds that what the Fund needs is achievement and, "To achieve, the IMF needs to refocus and deliver."

Four international experts on the wrap-up panel at the Institute conference expressed an even greater urgency for IMF reform. Barry Eichengreen (chapter 25) describes the Fund "as a rudderless ship adrift on a sea of liquidity. On none of the key issues does the institution or its principal shareholders have a clear, or a clearly articulated, position." Mohamed El-Erian (chapter 26) chooses different words but comes out in the same place: The IMF is losing relevance, there is no simple solution, and what it needs is a critical mass of reforms. Tommaso Padoa-Schioppa (chapter 27) argues that the Fund has drifted from its core mission of ensuring stability and has lost leverage because for many countries international liquidity is no longer scarce. Finally, Yu Yongding (chapter 28), while more reserved than the others, nevertheless agrees with C. Fred Bergsten (chapter 13) that the Fund has become weak and ineffective.

The Content of IMF Reform

On the content of IMF reform, the managing director's strategy document (IMF 2005k) is frequently eloquent in its diagnosis of the issues. In arguing for more effective surveillance, he calls for improvements in focus and context, "less cover-the-waterfront reporting on economies, more incisive analysis of specific weaknesses and distortions that risk crises and contagion or hinder adjustment to globalization, and more active Fund engagement in policy debates that shape public opinion and policy choices," including a revitalization of the IMF's International Monetary and Financial Committee (IMFC), which meets twice a year at the ministerial level and provides nonbinding guidance on IMF policies and activities.

On capital account liberalization, the managing director's report perceptively observes, "Financial globalization has both caused and been caused by the liberalization of the capital account." With respect to the Fund's role in addressing the many problems and challenges faced by low-income countries, he acknowledges "a consensus that the Fund should remain engaged in these areas" but asks "how best to do so, and to what degree?" Finally, with respect to governance, IMF quotas, and voice in the institution, he notes, "The current allocation puts this legitimacy [of the Fund as a universal institution] at risk in many regions. . . . In the view of too many, governance and ownership imbalances in the Fund now rival global current account imbalances. Neither imbalance is sustainable." However, on none of these issues does Managing Director de Rato put forward, or promise to put forward, concrete proposals. This lack of leadership is most notable in the area of IMF governance, where there is widespread agreement that actions are needed but no consensus about their content.

The communiqués of the IMFC, the Group of Seven (G-7), the Group of Ten (G-10), and the Group of Twenty-Four (G-24) issued at the time of the September 2005 IMF–World Bank annual meetings as well as the communiqué of the Group of Twenty (G-20) issued in mid-October all welcome the managing director's report and look forward to specific proposals.[3]

Almost all individual pronouncements in September 2005 by IMF governors and members of the IMFC emphasized the salience of the governance issues without suggesting any degree of consensus on appropriate solutions. There is a similar lack of consensus on IMF policies with respect to emerging-market economies. In addition, the managing director's report calls for a sharper delineation of the IMF's involvement with the Fund's low-income members, implying a substantial reorientation and scaling back of the financial and organizational resources devoted to the Fund's activities in this area, but the statements by finance ministers and central bank governors suggest less than full comprehension of his implication. In support of a more expansive vision of the IMF's role in low-income countries is the report's advocacy of intensified IMF involvement in the building of institutions and capacity in low-income countries. Such an increased emphasis would be likely to move the Fund into activities beyond its traditional core competencies on fiscal, monetary, exchange rate, and financial-sector policies; and IMF members may also underappreciate the implications of this suggestion.

The managing director's strategy document barely mentions exchange rates and omits entirely any discussion of the IMF's responsibilities in

---

3. The G-7 comprises Canada, France, Germany, Italy, Japan, the United Kingdom, and the United States. The G-10 grouping comprises the G-7 countries and also Belgium, the Netherlands, Sweden, and Switzerland. The G-24—formally the Intergovernmental Group of Twenty-Four on International Monetary Affairs and Development—comprises representatives of 24 Asian, African, Latin American, and Middle Eastern countries plus observers. The industrial-country members of the G-20 are the G-7 countries, Australia, and the country holding the EU presidency when not a European G-7 country; the nonindustrial-country members are Argentina, Brazil, China, India, Indonesia, Korea, Mexico, Russia, Saudi Arabia, South Africa, and Turkey.

this area; officials noted this omission in a number of statements at the time of the IMF–World Bank annual meetings. With respect to reports on "surveillance-only cases" of advanced and/or systemically important countries, the strategy document advocates discussing reasons why the Fund's advice is not accepted and what adaptations might deal with such concerns. A number of official commentators noted that this approach might usefully be applied to all members. A few also noted the omission of a broad treatment in the report of the IMF's lending activities aside from the mention of a few proposals that are under discussion and the controversial issue of the IMF's role in crisis resolution. Finally, although most officials have welcomed and praised the managing director's report, a few have commented that it lacks ambition or fails to recognize what one finance minister identifies as a need for organizational and cultural change in the institution.

Michel Camdessus (2005) evoked several noteworthy contrasts when he delivered the Per Jacobsson Foundation lecture two days after the Institute conference on IMF reform. Perhaps because he was liberated from the constraints of his former position as managing director, Camdessus presented a more comprehensive and provocative reform agenda covering the IMF's mission, its human and financial resources, and its governance; see box 1.2. He went beyond de Rato's strategy paper in arguing that the Fund should propose a bold initiative in the area of global imbalances such as organizing a new Plaza or Louvre agreement although, of course, the IMF was on the sidelines at those events. He said the IMF is and should be equipped to be an international lender of last resort and should expand its provision of financing to low-income members. Camdessus also advocated the introduction of population into the formula used to guide negotiations on the distribution of IMF quotas, and he called for a consolidated European chair in a smaller Executive Board. In an area not addressed by de Rato at all, Camdessus argued that the Fund should have significant periodic increases in its quota resources and should positively consider the resumption of allocations of special drawing rights (SDR).

An IMF Reform Package

The Institute's conference on IMF reform did not attempt to reach consensus on an IMF reform agenda. However, the elements of an overall strategy emerge from the conference and contemporaneous developments. A critical mass of reforms should encompass six components: governance, policies of systemically important countries, the central role of the Fund in external financial crises, refocused engagement with low-income countries, increased attention to capital account and financial-sector issues, and the case for additional financial resources.

Box 1.2   Michel Camdessus's reform agenda

Michel Camdessus (2005) gave the Per Jacobsson Lecture on September 25, 2005. He identified two key challenges for the IMF, on which he focused most of his attention, and for the other international financial institutions (IFIs) over the next 15 years: helping emerging-market countries advance more rapidly and helping the poorest countries reduce poverty. To meet these challenges, he laid out a three-part reform agenda for the IFIs: mission, human and financial resources, and governance. In the course of his remarks he put forward 20 separate proposals for IMF reform.

Under the heading of the IMF's mission, Camdessus called for strengthening surveillance and proposed reinforcing the IMF's message, in particular for the major countries, by submitting the preliminary conclusions of staff missions to a broader public debate within countries before the Executive Board reviews them. He argued for paying more attention to structural rigidities (including those in labor markets), demographic developments, and large accumulations of international reserves. He advocated a "bold initiative" by the IMF to deal with payments imbalances by structuring a cooperative effort along the lines of the Plaza (1985) and Louvre (1987) agreements, but this time with the IMF—not the G-7 or the G-20—at the center of the process.

With respect to mission, Camdessus proposed revisiting the issue of orderly capital account liberalization to learn the lessons of previous experience. Acknowledging that this process would take time, he argued that, in order to promote the process of capital account liberalization, the IMF should have the same kind of jurisdiction over the capital account transactions that it has over current account transactions. He belittled the Asian countries' experience with capital controls during the Asian financial crisis and warned against using controls to buy time as a substitute for the right policies. He argued that controls promote distortions and corruption and tend to favor the rich over the poor.

In the area of debt workouts, Camdessus proposed renewing the debate about a sovereign debt restructuring mechanism or its equivalent, with the essential feature that the IMF should be in the center of its design and operation. He argued that the globalized financial system needs a lender of last resort and said the IMF is equipped to play this role. He proposed confirming the Fund in this role. He also advocated equipping the IMF with the authority to create special drawing rights (SDR) on a contingency basis to deal with global liquidity squeezes; countries not caught up in the squeeze would advance their allocations of SDR to the Fund for its use in conditional lending programs.

Finally, under the heading of mission, he proposed fighting corruption by introducing ethical requirements into the education of future business and official

(box continues next page)

Box 1.2   Michel Camdessus's reform agenda   *(continued)*

leaders. He also argued it is essential for the IMF to support its poorest members by increasing their access to concessional financing from the IMF, improving the provision of financing to countries in postconflict situations or after economic shocks, and focusing the attention of the IMF and other IFIs on the scale of the annual transfer of real resources to the poorest countries.[1]

Under the heading of human and financial resources, Camdessus proposed expanding staff resources to equip the Fund properly to carry out new responsibilities for global financial stability and the oversight of financial markets and to reduce the "cloning syndrome" in IMF recruiting efforts by seeking staff with broader skills (outside of economics) and experience (inside of national governments). He strongly rejected the view that IMF quota resources are taxpayers' money and proposed significant periodic increases in quotas and a less doctrinaire attitude against allocations of SDR.

Under the heading of governance, Camdessus argued that "the legitimacy of the Bretton Woods Institutions is increasingly questioned" and advocated the creation of the decision-making council provided for in the IMF Articles of Agreement to give political guidance to the Fund alongside the technical guidance provided by the Executive Board. He would replace not only the consultative International Monetary and Financial Committee but also the "G-10, G-20, and other Gs," thus implying the G-7. With respect to voting shares and the Executive Board itself, he proposed introducing population into the quota formula, a single European chair with multiple alternates in the Executive Board, and a parallel consolidation of other chairs to produce a smaller and higher-caliber board. He noted that these steps would take time and argued that the Europeans should take the lead to put them in motion. With respect to the choice of management, he supported renouncing the special US and European roles in the selection processes for the heads of the Fund and the World Bank: The processes should be open and competitive.

Finally, he proposed that the annual G-8 leaders' meetings should be coupled each year with an extended meeting with leaders of the countries on the new council and presumably in the meantime with the leaders of the countries that are members of the IMFC, which would create a global governance group with more legitimacy than today's G-8 or G-20. He added one proviso: The meetings should be prepared by the IFIs and also should be attended by the UN secretary general and the heads of other relevant multilateral organizations.

---

1. The transfer of real resources to a country is conventionally defined as net long-term capital inflows plus net foreign direct and portfolio equity investment inflows plus grants minus associated net interest or income payments deflated by a relevant price index such as the country's export price index.

Substantial Progress on IMF Governance

Substantial progress on IMF governance is crucial to enhancing the Fund's legitimacy and restoring trust in the institution by the vast majority of member countries. Although there is widespread agreement on the need for progress on this component of IMF reform, there has been no movement to date. Action is needed in three areas: representation on the IMF Executive Board, realignment of IMF voting shares, and with somewhat less immediacy procedures to choose IMF management. Without concrete steps at least in the first two of these areas, all other efforts to reform and refurbish the IMF will be useless because the necessary broad international support for the Fund will wither away. The institution will become irrelevant to the promotion of global economic and financial stability.

On representation on the IMF Executive Board, the European Union should declare its intention over time to consolidate its representation into a single seat or at most two (one for euro area and one for non–euro area members of the European Union). To demonstrate the EU commitment to this objective, in the election of executive directors in the fall of 2006, Ireland, Poland, and Spain should agree to join EU-majority constituencies. This action would reduce the number of EU executive directors and alternate executive directors to a maximum of seven each, and it would free up two or three such seats for representatives from non-EU countries. In the election in the fall of 2008, the number of EU-majority seats should be reduced from seven to five—three appointed and two elected executive directors—freeing up two new constituencies and two more positions as executive directors and alternate executive directors, respectively. By 2010, EU representation should be reduced to two seats, with full consolidation coming at the point when the euro area encompasses the same group of countries as the European Union.

The United States has leverage over this process because an 85 percent majority vote is required prior to each biennial election of executive directors to prevent a contraction of the size of the Executive Board to 20 seats from the current 24 seats. Thus, the United States with 17 percent of the votes can block the continuation of the status quo. In chapter 9 of the conference volume, I caution that the United States should deploy this leverage very carefully, in part to ensure the continued representation of the 43 countries that are members of the four smallest constituencies in terms of voting share.[4]

Second, IMF voting shares must be substantially realigned to recognize better the economic and financial weight of key emerging-market countries in the global economy. It is not sustainable that the policies of the

---

4. The four smallest constituencies by size currently are represented by executive directors from Brazil, India, Argentina, and Equatorial Guinea.

IMF are determined principally by the votes of those countries that no longer need to borrow from the Fund when other countries, which may need to borrow from the institution, are positioned to provide financial support to its lending activities and should have more say over policies affecting those activities. The 24 traditional industrial countries, which never again are likely to need to borrow from the IMF, currently hold 60.3 percent of the votes in the institution. The other members are 22 emerging-market countries, as classified in chapter 2 of this policy analysis, with 20.4 percent of the votes, which may need to borrow from the IMF but can also supply significant financial resources to the Fund, and 138 other developing countries with 19.3 percent of the votes. The issue of voting shares involves principally reducing the combined share of the industrial countries by 10 or more percentage points and increasing the share of the emerging-market countries as a group.[5]

A possible interim solution to the quota and voting-share issue may lie in a combination of small ad hoc increases in a few countries' quotas in addition to small voluntary reallocations of quotas without an overall increase in the size of the Fund, thus avoiding a need to increase total quotas. A limited reduction in the US quota and voting share by less than one percentage point as a consequence of ad hoc quota increases in individual quotas plus an agreement by Canada, Japan, and the major European countries to reallocate portions of their existing quotas might free up a total of 4 percentage points of total quotas for reallocation. That amount could be distributed to the six large non-European countries with quotas that, although they are now in the top 30 in terms of size, have the largest proportional discrepancies (greater than 30 percent) between calculated and actual quota shares.[6] The six countries are Singapore, Korea, Malaysia, Thailand, China, and Mexico, in decreasing order of their percentage discrepancies.[7] As a result, the average percentage discrepancy for this group would be reduced from more than 100 percent to approximately 35 percent. Such an approach, however, would leave five discrepancies of more than 30 percent between calculated and actual quota shares within the EU group—Denmark, Ireland, Luxembourg, Spain, and potentially Turkey. Thus, the Europeans would come under internal pressure to negotiate some rebalancing within their nascent group even as they converge toward a single quota.

Such an interim solution even in the unlikely event that it could be negotiated would be viewed as inadequate by those countries that advocate

---

5. Reform of voting shares also involves rectifying some of the distortions that have developed in voting shares within these groups of countries.

6. Calculated quota shares are derived from formulas that have been used in the past to guide quota negotiations. The estimates presented in this paragraph are based on IMF (2004g).

7. The order of absolute discrepancies is Singapore, China, Korea, Mexico, Malaysia, and Thailand.

an overhaul of the quota formula and a fundamental redistribution of quota shares along with rearranging chairs on the IMF Executive Board.[8] Thus, a redistribution of voting shares in the IMF by a few percentage points via ad hoc adjustments or reallocation of quotas is unlikely to pass the test of credibility.

On the other hand, as I argue in chapter 9 of the conference volume, the time is not ripe for the United States to reduce its voting share significantly from its current 17 percent to less than 15 percent and give up voluntarily its capacity to block (veto) a few key decisions affecting the IMF as an institution. The United States, in particular the US Congress, lacks the confidence that other members of the Fund would step into the leadership vacuum that this would create. The risk would be a further US withdrawal from multilateralism.

It follows that a more comprehensive approach is needed. At a minimum, the Europeans would have to agree to give up a much larger share of their present collective quotas—at least six percentage points—based on the logic that membership in the European Monetary Union (EMU) reduces the theoretical need for EMU members and, in particular, countries that also are members of the euro area to borrow from the Fund. Alternatively and preferably, substantial adjustments in quota shares should occur across the board in the context of an increase in the overall size of the Fund of at least 50 percent, with the large emerging-market countries contributing the bulk of the new resources. This should be part of at least two steps of successive increases in total quotas that would be directed at achieving parity in the voting shares of the European Union and the United States.

This reallocation of quota shares in the context of successive increases in the overall size of the Fund would be aided by agreement upon a new simplified quota formula for use in guiding the process of adjustment. Agreement on a new quota formula is desirable. It is not essential. Decisions on the allocation of quota shares are essentially political. In light of this fact and because the G-20 includes most of the key countries, the G-20 should take the lead in this political process, including the negotiation of a revised, simplified quota formula. Optimists can take some comfort from the fact that the G-20 meeting in mid-October 2005 agreed on the need for "concrete progress" on quota reform by the time of the annual meetings in September 2006 and suggested that the G-20 itself would seek to identify principles that could be used in the 13th general review of quotas to be completed by January 2008.

---

8. The combined calculated quota share of the EU countries as a group is estimated as five and one-half percentage points higher than their actual combined share today. Moreover, the hypothetical four percentage points in downward adjustment in the combined quota share of the United States, Europe, Canada, and Japan would be about half as large as implied by Lorenzo Bini Smaghi (chapter 10 of the conference volume) and less than one-third of the adjustment that I consider in chapter 9.

Third, on the somewhat less pressing issue of procedures for choosing the IMF's management, the United States and the Europeans at last should recognize that their claims that only their citizens may be in the pool of potential leaders for the IMF and World Bank lack credibility and undermine the legitimacy of the Bretton Woods institutions. They should propose agreement in the IMFC and Development Committee, or by resolutions adopted by the boards of governors of the IMF and World Bank, on open and transparent procedures to pick the next managing director of the IMF and the next president of the World Bank (Kahler 2001; chapter 11 of the conference volume). The procedures should encompass (1) dropping the convention that the president of the World Bank should be a US citizen, that the IMF managing director should be a European, and that the first deputy managing director of the IMF should be a US citizen; (2) developing a list of requirements for the positions; (3) assembling a short list of candidates, possibly including internal candidates; and (4) putting in place an open vetting process.[9] The new procedures also should include principles for use in reviewing the performance of the incumbents as heads of the IMF and World Bank should they wish to be reelected for second terms in 2009 and 2010.

Finally, as in the past, the IMF in the future will need to be steered by a dedicated group of its most important members. This is a practical reality. However, the G-7 is no longer the appropriate steering committee for the world economy. It should be replaced by the G-20, preferably transformed into a Finance 16 (F-16)—the G-20 with a single EU seat—as advocated by C. Fred Bergsten (chapter 13). It is essential, in this regard, that IMF management and senior staff stop resisting the emergence of the G-20/F-16 as the steering committee for the world economy, which includes the IMF as one of its major institutions.

Policies of Systemically Important Members

Today the IMF is behind the curve on the central issue of the first decade of the 21st century: promoting macroeconomic and exchange rate adjustments. Moreover, the benign economic and financial conditions that have sustained those imbalances during the past few years are unlikely to persist. Unless the IMF as an institution can more effectively discharge its responsibilities for the identification and resolution of global imbalances and other systemic threats to global prosperity, it will become increasingly ignored. The performance of the global economy and financial system will suffer.

---

9. In this area of institutional governance, the IMF and World Bank lag substantially behind the World Trade Organization, the Organization for Economic Cooperation and Development, and UN agencies such as the United Nations Development Program in implementing more transparent leadership selection procedures.

The IMF must assert its role as a global umpire as well as develop stronger means to increase its leverage over the macroeconomic policies of systemically important countries. In its efforts to influence these countries' policies, the IMF management and staff should start with sound analysis and quiet persuasion. However, the Fund must employ more than those limited, though essential, tools. This component of IMF reform should include four elements.

First, the Fund should introduce into its consultations with systemically important countries an element of "naming and shaming" of specific countries. Article IV reviews of those countries' policies should be more precise about the measures that those countries should adopt to improve their economic performance and contribute to global economic and financial stability. For example, the IMF should not merely recommend that the United States reduce its budget deficit but also state by how much and over what time horizon. Similarly, the IMF should not only suggest that countries adopt more flexible exchange rate regimes when in fact their currencies should appreciate in effective terms but also state by how much they should appreciate. In addition, Article IV reviews should include sections on why the systemically important countries have not accepted the IMF's previous advice.[10] For the systemically important countries, all IMF surveillance and review documents should be made public.

Second, the IMF needs to establish an overall framework for its surveillance activities with respect to systemically important countries. To this end, the IMF should implement unilaterally a scaled-back version of the Williamson (chapter 6) proposal to use reference exchange rates to guide its surveillance activities. The reference exchange rates would be based on macroeconomic policies that are consistent with the achievement of external and internal balance in each of the countries. Absent an immediate buy-in by the relevant countries to Williamson's full proposal to use reference exchange rates to guide judgments on intervention policies and on the appropriateness of countries' macroeconomic and financial policies, the IMF management and staff should develop and publicize its own set of reference exchange rates. This initiative should not be excessively challenging because at least until recently IMF staff regularly produced similar reports and presented them to the IMF Executive Board.

Third, the Fund should embrace Morris Goldstein's triad of proposals (chapter 5): (1) issue a semiannual report on the exchange rate policies of members that should be based on the reference exchange-rate framework described above; (2) make more frequent use of its existing powers to conduct special or ad hoc consultations on members' exchange rate policies; and (3) review its existing guidelines for surveillance over members' exchange rate policies to see whether they need to be clarified or updated.

---

10. Managing Director de Rato (IMF 2005k) made a similar proposal for the advanced or industrial countries; it should be applied to all systemically important countries.

Fourth, as a bold initiative to implement the second Goldstein proposal, the IMF should embark upon a collective consultation with the major Asian economies as a group—including at least China, Hong Kong, India, Japan, Korea, Malaysia, Singapore, Thailand, and on an informal basis Taiwan—about their macroeconomic and exchange rate policies. Each of these countries follows, or has followed in the recent past, a policy of heavily managing its exchange rate vis-à-vis the US dollar. The IMF (2005m) estimates a collective 2005 current account surplus of $215 billion for these countries or almost one-third of the IMF's estimate of the US current account deficit. Individually, the leaders of each economy look closely at their Asian neighbor's policies when setting their own exchange rate policy. Thus, modifications in the policies of these countries as a group are at the core of the resolution of global macroeconomic imbalances.

Central Role of the Fund in External Financial Crises

The IMF remains bedeviled by philosophical disputes about the scale and scope of its lending activities. These disputes distract the institution from its role as the global lender of final resort. This component of the IMF reform agenda should include three elements.

First, members of the Fund should reaffirm the central role of the IMF in international financial crises, including through its potentially large-scale lending activities. Unless the IMF distances itself from ideological preoccupations with excessive crisis lending and moral hazard concerns, the Fund will go into eclipse as an international crisis lender and the international community will lose its leverage over antisocial national economic policies.[11] Note that if the quota shares of the large emerging-market countries are increased as advocated in my agenda, those countries will be supplying the bulk of the additional financial resources for the IMF to lend. This shift in responsibility would be consistent with the original intent of the revolving character of IMF resources.

Second, in cases requiring debt restructurings, in particular those involving a sovereign default to private creditors, the Fund should embrace the proposal by William Cline (chapter 14 of the conference volume). To

---

11. Observers and critics from European countries, in particular, fail to recognize the implications of a world that differs from when their countries faced balance of payments crises in the early 1950s through the middle of the 1970s. Those countries during that period received large amounts of financial support from the IMF often supplemented by special bilateral financial arrangements even in the context of the protection offered by their capital controls. No one raised a peep about moral hazard at that time. Today, no sensible observer or critic advocates returning to a world of comprehensive capital controls. As a consequence, the potential need for the IMF as a lender of final resort has increased, not decreased.

guide the debt renegotiation process, the IMF should establish and publicize its estimates of high, central, and low "resource envelopes" for the country. Such resource envelopes would indicate the amounts of financial resources the country could reasonably be expected to devote to external debt service, under a range of assumptions about external conditions and the country's policies, in order to achieve a sustainable trajectory for servicing the country's debts.

If at the request of the member country the Fund's involvement with the debt renegotiation process stops there, the international financial community should be informed. At that point, the IMF additionally should be required to tell the borrower the parameters of a proposal for debt restructuring that is not only sustainable but also comprehensive in that it is likely to be embraced by a very high proportion of the country's external creditors. Preferably, all countries should welcome the IMF's central involvement in sovereign debt negotiations because the Fund is positioned to provide a public good in the form of coordination in the face of a market failure of coordination and uncertain amounts of asymmetric information. In complicated cases, neither the country (nor its advisers) nor its private creditors are in a position to supply unbiased information. The Fund should play this coordination role regardless of how extensive and detailed a code of conduct the parties may have accepted in advance to govern their financial relationships.

In the post-2001 Argentine case, none of the above procedures was in place. Therefore, it is appropriate that the IMF review and clarify its policy on lending to a member that is not maintaining its debt-service payments to its external private creditors—IMF lending into arrears—to provide clearer guidance to members and markets.

Third, with respect to new facilities, the IMF (management and members) should keep an open mind. Tito Cordella and Eduardo Levy Yeyati (chapter 17) propose a country insurance facility in the IMF for which a member would prequalify and receive automatic access to an adequate amount of finance to deal with an external financial crisis without requiring major changes in its fiscal stance. Using their tight parameterization, this facility will make only a marginal contribution to dealing with presumptive liquidity crises. That fact should not preclude experimentation with such mechanisms in the spirit of modernizing the IMF for the 21st century.

In addition, the facility proposed by Michael Mussa (chapter 21) to reschedule IMF claims in exceptional and well-defined cases should be established. This proposal should be implemented before the global economic and financial environment becomes less benign than it has been for the past three years and before the next Argentine type of case develops, for example in connection with Indonesia, Turkey, or Uruguay—three representative countries with sizable outstanding liabilities to the IMF and substantial sovereign and external debt ratios.

Refocused Engagement with Low-Income Members

Poverty reduction in all its dimensions, from raising standards of living to defeating the scourge of disease, is one of the major challenges of the 21st century. However, it does not follow from this fact that the IMF should be transformed into a relatively ill-equipped development finance institution as some of its caring but less thoughtful members appear to advocate. The IMF's mission is to promote maximum sustainable global growth and financial stability. If it is successful, the Fund's low-income members will benefit more than any other group. Low-income members, when they face short-term balance of payments problems, also should receive temporary financial assistance from the Fund, possibly on subsidized terms.

However, the Fund should be selective and focused in its engagement with its low-income members, ready to assist them in areas of its comparative advantage, reluctant to add to their debts, and respectful of the skills and opportunities offered by institutions centrally involved with development issues. The Fund cannot successfully be all things to all countries; that violates the law of comparative advantage. It is important that the Fund's members and management recognize its limitations.

Moving forward on this component of IMF reform will not be easy although hints at a convergence of views are encouraging. Political leaders in low-income countries want all the financial assistance they can get. However, some of those leaders now recognize that too much help can create distractions and policy overload. This critique is implicit in Steven Radelet's review (chapter 20) of the IMF's engagement with poststabilization, low-income countries. Political leaders in traditional donor countries, in particular finance ministers, trust the Fund and value the soundness of IMF policy advice more than the advice of the traditional development institutions; they also have greater confidence that the Fund is more circumspect in its disbursements. Moreover, political leaders in many member countries other than the low-income countries point to their own development and poverty problems that tend to be neglected, as discussed by Kemal Derviş and Nancy Birdsall (chapter 16).

The answer to the question of the appropriate depth of IMF involvement with its low-income members lies in partnership and a thoughtful division of labor, in particular, between the Fund and the World Bank. IMF Managing Director de Rato and World Bank President Paul Wolfowitz have committed themselves to yet another attempt to establish a framework for cooperation across Northwest Washington's 19th Street.

The first step is to recognize that all past efforts have been halfhearted and failed. The Fund is perceived by the Bank as an organization populated by know-it-all elitists, and the Bank is perceived by the Fund as an organization populated by uncoordinated do-gooders, each with a personal solution to the multiple challenges of development but with no appreciation of budget constraints—financial, political, or administrative.

Both perceptions contain kernels of truth. Thus, the Fund should develop a culture that says the Bank is better than we are in many important areas and vice versa.

A concrete action for the IMF reform agenda is the Radelet proposal (chapter 20) that the World Bank invite the Fund to provide the assessments of members' macroeconomic policies in the Bank's Country Policy and Institutional Assessment (CPIA) system.[12] This proposal could be built on by requiring that all World Bank loan documents include IMF assessments of the member's macroeconomic policies and debt-service capacity. On the other side, no longer should negative staff assessments along with their implicit endorsement by the IMF executive directors be sufficient to block substantial access to World Bank and regional development bank resources. Finally, the members of the IMF should reject Managing Director de Rato's suggestion that the IMF should become more actively involved in institution building; this is an area where the IMF generally does not have a comparative advantage.

If the IMF were to refocus its engagement with low-income countries on its core areas of comparative advantage—policy advice on macroeconomic and financial policies, surveillance, and temporary balance of payments assistance—the result would be a substantial reduction in lending through the IMF to these countries.[13] Lending to countries eligible for Poverty Reduction and Growth Facility (PRGF) programs will be reduced in any case. At least 18 countries will have 100 percent of their debts to the IMF written off, and those countries should not be eligible for new IMF loans in the immediate future. Another group of the low-income countries can be expected to take advantage of the new Policy Support Instrument, which involves IMF support for a country's policies but no commitment to lend to it. Finally, if the members of the IMF also were to embrace Managing Director de Rato's call for a substantial cutback in IMF involvement in the development of Poverty Reduction Strategy Papers, the net result would be a substantial scaling back of PRGF-type activities and the de facto transfer of many of those activities to the World Bank.

Attention to the Capital Account and the Financial Sector

Capital account and financial-sector issues are central to the IMF's role in the 21st century. Technology, demography, and policy have converged to

---

12. The CPIA system is the World Bank's internal mechanism used to provide guidance on the scale of its lending to individual members. In the past, countries' performances have been grouped by quintile and published. Starting in 2006, the individual country assessments will be made public.

13. Today, most IMF lending to low-income countries eligible for Poverty Reduction and Growth Facility programs involves resources that have been lent voluntarily to the IMF, not its own quota-based resources.

stimulate and release unprecedented global flows of capital. These international forces mirror and build upon comparable developments within countries.

As a component of the IMF reform agenda, members should exploit an emerging consensus and upgrade the IMF's capacity to provide policy advice and analysis on members' external and internal financial sectors. IMF advice should not be limited to destination countries, in part because many of those countries increasingly are also source countries and in particular because the principal source countries need advice as well (Williamson 2005).

An amendment of the IMF Articles of Agreement to establish and clarify the IMF's role with respect to the capital account is not essential at this time; the Fund can do its job without one. On the other hand, IMF members should accept, at least implicitly, that full capital account liberalization is an appropriate long-run objective for all member countries. The consensus on this proposition is greater today than was the consensus in 1944 favoring current account liberalization. An amendment to clean up the IMF Articles can wait until this consensus is more widely recognized and embraced. Meanwhile, the IMF should shape its policies and expertise accordingly.

Finally, consistent with the principle of comparative advantage, the IMF should scale back its role in providing advice and technical assistance to its members on financial-sector issues and transfer much of this activity to the World Bank following the formula sketched out above for macroeconomic policy assessments for World Bank borrowers. Under this model, the Fund would concentrate on financial-sector assessments and analyses of the vulnerability of its members to financial-sector weaknesses and shocks such as those faced by East Asian countries in the late 1990s: excessive reliance on short-term capital inflows, inadequate attention to currency mismatches, and weak financial-sector supervision. The IMF should leave most technical assistance in this area to the World Bank with two exceptions: first a country receiving IMF financial support and where the technical assistance directly contributes to the achievement of the program's objectives, and second, a specific request as a result of a surveillance recommendation.

The report of the McDonough Group (IMF 2005l), formally known as the Review Group on the Organization of Financial Sector and Capital Markets Work at the Fund, reportedly does not consider this option for reforming the Fund's work on the financial sector. The McDonough Group did not talk with the Bank. On the other hand, Managing Director de Rato is right (IMF 2005k; chapter 3 of the conference volume) to point to the need to refocus the Fund on financial-sector analysis as its key contribution to international financial stability in the 21st century. In this respect, the McDonough Group's report apparently makes clear that the Fund has a long way to go if it is to be effective. Reform must start at the leadership level.

Additional Financial Resources

The IMF will not need additional financial resources in 2006. However, IMF credit outstanding to all members increased by more than 50 percent from the end of 2000 through the end of 2003—a period of global recession. Credit to its emerging-market members in May 2005 was still more than 20 percent above the level at the end of 2000 despite overwhelmingly benign economic and financial conditions during the past two years that have facilitated large net repayments to the Fund. Wise observers caution that those benign conditions are coming to an end, and the demand for external financial support from the IMF is likely to rise.

Statements by US officials and officials of many other industrial countries that the IMF does not now need additional financing convey the implicit message that the IMF will never need (or deserve) additional financing. That message is wrong. It was right to increase the IMF's financial resources in 1998; IMF credit outstanding increased by one-third during the subsequent five fiscal years. Moreover, nothing in the scale of the improvements of the global economic and financial system during the past decade supports an abrupt decline in the scale of IMF financing relative to the nominal expansion of the world economy and financial system; see table 6.1 and the associated discussion in chapter 6 of this policy analysis.

When messages about expanding IMF resources are couched in the language of domestic budgetary debates—the way to close down programs is to starve the beasts of financial support—they are further debilitating to the Fund and to perceptions of its role in the global financial system. Officials of industrial countries should modify their messages, state that they will support an increase in IMF quotas when the case is made, acknowledge that the case may well be made before January 2008 when the 13th review of IMF quotas is scheduled to be completed, and start to lay the groundwork with their parliaments for an increase in IMF quotas at some point during the next three to five years. As noted above in connection with the issue of IMF governance, a decision in early 2008 to increase IMF quotas might well be essential to achieving substantial progress on that component of IMF reform.

In the meantime, the IMF should put in place a mechanism so it can borrow from the private market as a temporary supplement to its quota resources as supported by Desmond Lachman (chapter 23). The IMF has this power without an amendment to its Articles of Agreement. A debate on this issue should proceed in parallel with a serious discussion about how to provide the Fund with a stable source of income to finance its nonlending activities. The IMF's expanding nonlending activities are financed principally from its lending operations, which appear to be on a downtrend and, in any case, are cyclical in nature. This important issue is discussed by Mohamed El-Erian (chapter 26).

Final Comments

The first three components of the six-part agenda for IMF reform offered here—governance, systemically important countries, and external financial crises—are time critical. Concrete progress on IMF governance is necessary to underpin the relevance of the IMF's role with respect to the second two components. The last three—low-income countries, the capital account and financial sector, and IMF resources—are less time critical because, unless the triad of principal components is successfully confronted, how the IMF performs on the other components will not matter. The IMF will become an ill-equipped development institution, offering advice of limited global relevance and without the need to supplement its financial resources because, in effect, it will be in the business of administering grants to low-income countries to support macroeconomic policy adjustments.

Reforming the IMF to enable it to discharge its core mission of promoting international economic growth and financial stability in the 21st century is urgent if the Fund is not going to sink into irrelevance. No one can predict accurately the tipping point at which the IMF loses the support of its 20 to 30 systemically most important members and thereby loses its capacity to provide financing to those countries if they should need financial support, or to support their other global economic and financial objectives even if they should not. However, at some point—and on the present trajectory I suspect that point is not too distant—enough IMF members will conclude that the institution as currently constituted is not sufficiently relevant to their national interests, and they will cease to support the Fund and its provision of international public goods.

Therefore, the IMF needs a proactive reform agenda, an agenda with more precision and promise than that put forward by Managing Director de Rato. The agenda must contain a critical mass of reforms covering the six components listed in this chapter. It must address the interests of all members. It must be a package that provides something for each country even if each country does not get everything it wants and has to swallow some elements it would prefer to leave out.

The agenda outlined above does not require an amendment to the IMF Articles of Agreement at this time or in the next few years. On the other hand, if over the next year or two a consensus emerges to increase IMF quotas in 2008 and, much more important, if agreement can be reached on a more ambitious reform package than the one sketched out here, a fifth amendment of the IMF Articles of Agreement might be part of that package.[14]

---

14. The fifth amendment might include (1) an increase in basic votes, discussed in chapter 4 of this policy analysis, (2) authorization for special, temporary SDR allocations to help the IMF deal with external financial crises, discussed by Lachman (chapter 23 of the conference volume), (3) adjustments in the provisions of the current Articles to facilitate the consolida-

The rationale for the proposed agenda for IMF reform is to create a better Fund to better serve the global community. The Fund needs reforming, and the management of the Fund recognizes that fact. However, IMF member governments must commit the necessary political capital to make IMF reform a reality.

tion of EU representation in the IMF, which I discuss in chapter 9, even though substantial if not total consolidation of EU representation could be accomplished without an amendment, and (4) establishing a framework for IMF membership and relations with regional monetary arrangements, discussed by C. Randall Henning (chapter 7). Presumably such an expanded package would include a commitment from the US government to push for passage of the Fourth Amendment of the Articles authorizing a special, one-time allocation of SDR principally to those members, including Russia and most of the former Soviet Union and Eastern Europe, that were not members of the IMF in 1970–72 or 1979–81 when SDR were allocated. The United States promoted the amendment, 131 members of the IMF with 77 percent of the weighted votes have ratified it, and the IMFC routinely calls for the completion of the ratification process, which cannot happen without US action.

2

IMF Activities and Reform Efforts

IMF Managing Director Rodrigo de Rato stated on June 10, 2005, "The IMF's mandate is directed squarely at the promotion and maintenance of macroeconomic and financial stability, both in individual countries and at the international level."[1] Many other officials and observers use similar words to describe the Fund's role. For example, Secretary of the Treasury John Snow, addressing the Fund's IMFC in April 2005, stated, "The IMF's mission is clear—to foster international monetary cooperation and balance of payments adjustment to support international financial stability and economic growth" (Snow 2005). Nevertheless, not everyone accepts this broad articulation of the Fund's mission and therein lies a major challenge the IMF faces: a lack of understanding and support for the organization and its core objective of promoting global economic and financial stability.

Mandate

One reason why some challenge the view that the Fund's mission is to promote economic and financial stability is that Article I of the Articles of Agreement of the International Monetary Fund does not contain a clear statement of the IMF's purposes relevant to the international financial system of the 21st century. Article I speaks of

- promotion of international monetary cooperation,
- facilitation of the expansion and balanced growth of world trade,

---

1. Remarks delivered at the IESE Business School, University of Navarra, Madrid.

- maintenance of high levels of employment and real income,

- promotion of exchange stability,

- temporary provision of financial resources to correct balance of payments positions without resorting to measures destructive of national or international prosperity, and

- lessening the degree of disequilibrium in the international balance of payments of members.

Article I, thus, establishes macroeconomic stability and growth as central to the Fund's statutory purposes. However, the capital account crises that have been a major preoccupation of the IMF and much of its membership during the past decade have pointed in addition to the importance of maintaining financial stability in order to achieve macroeconomic stability and growth. IMF Article I does not explicitly mention financial stability as an objective. Article IV does state, "The essential purpose of the international monetary system is to provide a framework that facilitates the exchange of goods, services, and capital among countries and that sustains sound economic growth, and that a principal objective is the continuing development of the orderly underlying conditions that are necessary for economic and financial stability." Article IV also lists obligations of members in their policies devoted toward these ends. On the other hand, Article VI enjoins members from using IMF resources "to meet a large or sustained outflow of capital" and endorses the use of controls to regulate capital movements. In today's world the Article VI prescriptions are anachronisms, but an attempt in the late 1990s to remove these contradictions and to update the IMF Articles of Agreement in this area to enshrine the liberalization of capital movements as one of the purposes of the Fund and to establish the IMF's authority over capital account issues foundered on the political and economic disagreements that surrounded the IMF's handling of the East Asian financial crises. At the same time, Article IV adopted in the 1970s clearly provides the Fund with surveillance responsibilities with respect to capital flows and financial systems and the scope to advise and admonish members on their policies in those areas.

There is an irony in much of this. On the one hand, many observers who want to scale back the IMF in dealing with international financial crises point to the exponential growth of private international financial markets to justify their position. They certainly have some of their facts right, but the expansion of access to these markets is relevant only to a small fraction of the nonindustrial countries that are members of the Fund, and the access of these countries to international financial markets is far from continuous. Thus, some observers see the evolution of international financial markets as a substitute for the Fund. Others see that evolution as causing increased international financial instability that the IMF should be better equipped to address.

In fact, most officials and observers do include domestic financial system stability among the core activities of the IMF along with monetary, fiscal, and exchange rate policies. They link those activities to the IMF's prevention and management of international financial crises. For example, Executive Director Kevin Lynch (2005), of Canada, testified before the Canadian parliament that "[t]he Fund's mission is to prevent international financial crises if possible and, if not, then remediate them quickly and efficiently." Even critics of the IMF who advocate a narrowing of the IMF's mandate stress the importance of its role with respect to financial systems and capital movements. For example, Allan Meltzer (2005) stated, "The IMF's responsibility should remain the maintenance of global *financial* stability."[2] Charles Calomiris (2005) stated, "The legitimate current purpose of the Fund is to help to smooth capital market and exchange rate adjustments involving investment by developed countries in emerging-market countries."

The IMF's membership at 184 is close to universal, smaller than the United Nations by only seven countries.[3] Despite disagreements about the scope of its mission, the IMF is an institution of global governance. It is ultimately responsible to governments that contribute to its financing and give direction to its policies. Nongovernmental organizations (NGOs) and other national and international interest groups are not always pleased with or fully accepting of this reality because this fact deprives them of access and influence. At the same time, governmental institutions are controversial because of a lack of consensus about the appropriate role of government today.[4] Institutions of global governance, or institutions of international collective decision making, generate even more controversy.[5] Governments and their institutions are designed to provide public goods, for example in the international context to cope with cross-country externalities. Economists often appeal to market failures to make the case for government or international collective action. The problem is that economists do not agree about the nature of the market's failures or about whether proposed cures for those failures are likely to improve the functioning of the financial system. Moreover, political leaders do not always listen to their economic advisers.

The IMF has evolved during its 60 years. The Fund started life as the manager of the Bretton Woods international monetary system based on

---

2. Emphasis added.

3. The seven countries are Andorra, Cuba, North Korea, Liechtenstein, Monaco, Nauru, and Tuvalu.

4. Boughton (2005) examines the evolution of the IMF and the challenges associated with both its effective operation and its continued maturation.

5. See Bryant (2003) for an admirable and informative attempt to describe efforts to establish institutions of cross-border finance and international governance as well as to prescribe pragmatic ways to move forward.

fixed exchange rates designed to avoid the pitfalls and internationally antisocial policies of the 1930s. Following the collapse of the Bretton Woods system and revision of its Articles of Agreement in the mid-1970s, the Fund became known as a firefighter dealing with the international debt problems of the 1980s, the facilitator of the economic transformation of countries in Eastern Europe and the former Soviet Union at the end of the 1980s, a partner in the struggle against global poverty in the early 1990s, and an instrument in the prevention and management of capital account crises in the late 1990s.

This evolution itself has been controversial. A recent example of the Fund's evolution has been its increasing involvement in the area of abuse of the international financial system. In the late 1990s, for example, it was called upon to review the compliance of offshore financial centers with a number of internationally accepted standards. After September 11, 2001, the Fund acquired an enhanced role in the scrutiny of compliance with standards covering anti–money laundering and combating the financing of terrorism.

For some observers outside and inside the IMF, the expansion of the Fund's activities is the pragmatic response by an established and respected institution to the changing needs of its members and the changing character of the international financial system. According to this view, it is more efficient and effective to use an existing institution to meet new challenges than it is to create new institutions.

For others, the evolution of the IMF represents nefarious mission creep, a bureaucratic effort to expand the institution's scope and influence. Thus, Michael Bordo and Harold James (2000) describe a process of supply response to perceived, but questionable in their view, market failures and the demands of IMF members for help to cope with them. They advocate a narrowing of the scope of the IMF's activities to establishing data standards, dealing with short-term liquidity problems, and providing information to markets via surveillance.

At the other end of the ideological spectrum, Sarah Babb and Ariel Buira (2005) bemoan what they see as an increase in the discretion exercised by the IMF management and staff, the absence of rules, and a tendency toward "mission push" by the United States and other members of the G-7. They advocate a more rules-based organization with increased transparency and accountability, increased financial assistance associated with fewer and narrower conditions, and a reworked governance and voting structure, including the elimination of the US capacity to block (veto) some decisions.

The IMF has evolved, but the role of the IMF as an institution of collective global governance has always been limited. Timothy Geithner, in June 10, 2004, remarks before the Bretton Woods Committee on the subject of the Bretton Woods institutions and the 21st century, aptly described its continuing dilemma:

The Fund, from its inception, was burdened by a mismatch between the aspirations of its architects and the authority and instruments they gave the institution to pursue those ambitions. Its authority over the policies of its members was limited. Its resources were small, and the facilities established to deploy those resources were modest relative to the problems they were designed to address.

Notwithstanding concerns within and outside the Fund about mission creep, there is broad agreement on the core activities of the Fund: fiscal policies, monetary policies, and exchange rate policies. As mentioned above, the financial sector joined this triumvirate about 10 years ago, and this has been an area of rapid expansion as well as considerable accomplishment, but not without its critics and controversies.

This extension of the Fund's core activities to the financial sector has been somewhat problematic. First, as noted, it is not well based in the Articles of Agreement. Second, the Fund shares jurisdiction in this area with the World Bank, which often has a longer-term perspective on financial-sector issues, a different relationship with its members, and naturally a different set of views about what should be done and when. Third, the Fund is not a financial supervisor. The Fund was the principal drafter of only three of the dozen internationally recognized standards and codes that have been endorsed by the IMF and the World Bank in connection with their Reports on Observance of Standards and Codes (ROSCs).[6] The Fund's principal and important role has been in the area of compliance with existing standards and codes.

In practice, of course, the IMF is now heavily involved in financial-sector and related capital market issues in its analyses and its country programs. The broad membership of the Fund has grudgingly accepted this involvement as it argues about details. For example, how broad and intrusive should be the examinations of countries' compliance with international standards on anti–money laundering and combating the financing of terrorism? To what extent should the results of those examinations be factored into structural conditions in programs receiving IMF (or World Bank) financial support?

The United States and the rest of the G-7 continue to press the IMF in this area. Acting Under Secretary of the Treasury for International Affairs Randal Quarles (2005), of the United States, stated in testimony, "The IMF needs to integrate more fully capital market and financial-sector analysis into the daily life of the Fund." In partial response to similar views expressed in the context of commenting on the Fund's own medium-term

---

6. The IMF has been principally responsible for drafting the standards on data transparency, fiscal transparency, and monetary and financial policy transparency. Various international standards-setting bodies had principal responsibility for drafting eight of the other nine standards; for example, in the case of the banking supervision standard, the Basel Committee on Banking Supervision undertook this responsibility after much prodding from many quarters. The World Bank was the principal drafter of the standard on insolvency and creditor rights.

strategic review, Managing Director de Rato in June 2005 formed a working group under the direction of William McDonough to provide an independent perspective on how well the Fund has organized its financial-sector analysis.

Tools and Activities

To carry out its mission, the IMF uses three principal tools: surveillance, lending, and technical assistance.[7] These activities contribute to the production of two basic products: policy advice and financing.

Surveillance operates at several levels. At the core are the essentially annual Article IV consultations with individual countries on their economic and financial policies and prospects, including "firm surveillance" over their exchange rate policies. These reviews cover the full range of macroeconomic policies and performance and include, as well, microeconomic and structural policies and issues such as trade policies, labor market policies, and pension systems. Of the members, 88 percent have agreed, at least once, to allow the resulting written assessments to be published. Also of the members, 97 percent have agreed, at least once, to the publication of a public information notice (PIN) that summarizes the staff's and the Executive Board's views of the country's policies and performance after an Article IV consultation (IMF 2005g, table 1).[8]

Individual countries may also volunteer for reviews of their financial sectors and associated risks and vulnerabilities.[9] In addition, members may volunteer for assessments of their compliance with the 12 principal international standards, codes, and principles.[10] The 1999 initiative to involve the IMF and the World Bank in reviews of compliance with international standards was a major component of the effort to strengthen the international financial architecture. It is intended to aid countries in their reform efforts, to aid the Fund and Bank in their work with countries, and to in-

---

7. The IMF's research activities are an omitted tool from this standard list. Since the institution's founding, those activities have played a major role in establishing the Fund's policy credibility. That tool should not be neglected.

8. Publication is a voluntary decision by the member country; a few countries have not permitted publication every year after first permitting publication.

9. The Financial Sector Assessment Program (FSAP) is conducted jointly with the World Bank. As of August 31, 2005, 50 percent of IMF members had completed FSAPs (IMF 2005g, table 1). Another 17 percent had FSAPs under way or their participation in the program had been confirmed. The FSAP also forms the basis for confidential Financial Sector Stability Assessments (FSSAs) that look at the vulnerability of the macroeconomy to financial shocks and the vulnerability of the financial system to macroeconomic shocks.

10. The resulting documents are ROSCs. The reports consist of various modules, and a country may voluntarily agree to publish the reports. As of August 31, 2005, the reports on 74 percent of the completed modules had been published.

form market participants. At a recent review of the initiative (IMF 2005d), executive directors were "broadly satisfied with the initiative's effectiveness"—faint praise indeed—but expressed disappointment that market participants' use of the ROSCs remains low. However, Rachel Glennerster and Yongseok Shin (2003) find statistical evidence that the market rewards transparent countries, including those countries that comply with international standards and codes, with lower spreads. Charis Christofides, Christian Mulder, and Andrew Tiffin (2003) in a careful study reach a similar conclusion with respect to both spreads and ratings. However, the size of the effects provides limited leverage over compliance with codes. Moreover, empirical work in this area is in its infancy (Goldstein 2005a).

The Fund also conducts regional surveillance, for example of the euro area. It conducts global surveillance in the form of its semiannual reviews of the global economic outlook and of the global financial system.[11] In addition, the IMF staff prepares special reviews for meetings of various international groups such as the G-7 finance ministers and central bank governors for their meetings three times a year, for meetings of the deputies and the finance ministers of the Asia-Pacific Economic Cooperation (APEC) forum, and for meetings of the G-20 finance ministers and central bank governors.[12]

IMF lending takes place through a number of arrangements and facilities. The bread-and-butter Stand-By Arrangement (SBA) is designed to provide financing for members to help them deal with short-term balance of payments financing problems. The Extended Fund Facility (EFF) is intended to provide financing for members with longer-term balance of payments and structural problems. The Supplemental Reserve Facility (SRF) is used to supplement the regular balance of payments financing by providing larger amounts for shorter maturities and at higher interest rates in connection with "capital account crises."[13] The Compensatory Financing Facility (CFF) covers shortfalls in goods and services export earnings or increases in the cost of cereal imports that are temporary and caused by events beyond a member's control. Under the same heading is emergency assistance associated with natural disasters and postconflict situations. Finally, the Fund has a Poverty Reduction and Growth Facility (PRGF) that makes longer-term low-interest loans to low-income countries with structural balance of payments problems.[14] Countries eligible to

---

11. The associated published reports are the highly regarded *World Economic Outlook* and *Global Financial Stability Report*.

12. These documents are not published and probably should be.

13. In capital account crises, macroeconomic policies are reasonably sound and current account deficits are small, but a country faces a sudden reduction or reversal in capital inflows.

14. The PRGF was established in 1999; it replaced the Enhanced Structural Adjustment Facility (ESAF) that had been created in 1987.

borrow under the PRGF are those that are also eligible to borrow from the World Bank Group under its International Development Association (IDA) window. The Poverty Reduction Strategy Papers (PRSPs) in principle are prepared by the borrowing country as the basis for PRGF lending and are reviewed by the Executive Boards of both the Fund and the Bank.

The IMF also provides technical assistance to its members, normally free of charge. The technical assistance is intended to strengthen a country's institutional capacities in the areas of the IMF's expertise, such as central banking. This major activity absorbs a substantial portion of the IMF's financial and human resources. The activity is generally only loosely linked to IMF lending programs, actual or potential. Most of the technical assistance is financed out of the IMF's own resources, but about one-third is financed by contributions from its members. In fiscal year 2004, the IMF's share of the cost of its technical assistance absorbed 23 percent of the gross administrative budget, or $190 million, and about 700 person-years (IMF-IEO 2005b). Approximately 70 percent of the technical assistance goes to low-income countries with per capita incomes of less than $1,000 per year.[15]

In addition to these three core tools, some observers include poverty reduction as a fourth, although one might more reasonably consider it a potential goal.[16] The reduction of poverty in low-income countries is certainly an activity to which the IMF devotes a large amount of staff resources.[17] Under the PRGF, 78 countries are potentially eligible to borrow from the IMF. As of May 31, 2005, 62 countries (four-fifths of those eligible) had PRGF credit outstanding from the IMF.[18] The PRGF credit outstanding accounted for 73 percent of all IMF credit outstanding as of that date. Thus, poverty reduction is a major objective of IMF activity today. For example, 8 of the 33 pages in Managing Director de Rato's report to the April 2005 IMFC on the IMF's policy agenda dealt with IMF support for low-income members (IMF 2005f).

---

15. An evaluation of the revenue and expenses of the IMF's expanding operations is beyond the scope of this study and the expertise of its author, although I touch on it in chapter 6 on financial resources. Nevertheless, this is a major issue and is linked to other issues such as the amount of IMF lending and how the IMF finances its routine activities.

16. For example, Lynch (2005) stated that the IMF's tool kit has "four core components: surveillance, lending, capacity building, and poverty reduction."

17. The resources for PRGF lending are borrowed from countries and institutions generally at market-related interest rates. The terms of the lending to the PRGF borrowers (0.5 percent per year with repayments semiannually starting 5½ years and ending 10 years after disbursement) are in turn subsidized through donations and the IMF's own resources.

18. Table 2.5 shows 81 percent of PRGF-eligible countries were borrowers because I have classified India, technically PRGF eligible, as an emerging-market country in that table and other tables in this chapter.

Facts about the IMF and Its Lending

It is useful to look at some data on the IMF's evolution as an international monetary institution. Shortly after the IMF was founded in 1945 it had 40 members.[19] Thirty years later its membership had tripled to 127 members. An additional 57 members joined during the following 30 years to make up the current membership of 184.[20] The membership consists of 24 industrial countries, 77 countries that are now eligible to borrow from the PRGF, 22 countries that we have classified somewhat arbitrarily as emerging-market countries, and 61 other developing countries; see table 2.1.[21]

Table 2.2 provides a summary of the composition of the IMF's membership in 2005 and in 1975 by category of country and region of the world. By category of country, the largest increases were in what are now PRGF-eligible countries (28) and other developing countries (23). By region of the world, the largest increases were in Europe (27), principally in Eastern Europe and the former Soviet Union, Asia (12), and Africa (12).

More relevant than the evolution of the characteristics of the members of the IMF are the trends in patterns in the number of members that borrowed from the Fund over this 30-year period. Table 2.3 shows the distribution of the *number* of members with credit outstanding at the end of five-year periods from 1975 to 2005.[22] In 1975 and 1980, industrial countries

---

19. At the Bretton Woods conference in 1944, it was anticipated the IMF would have 45 founding members. However, the Union of Soviet Socialist Republics never joined, and Australia, Haiti, Liberia, and New Zealand delayed in joining. Three of the remaining founding members later withdrew: Czechoslovakia, Cuba, and Poland.

20. Twenty-five of the new members were from Eastern Europe and the former Soviet Union. Most of the remaining new members were small island nations, some having just received their independence. There were also a few African countries such as Mozambique, Namibia, and Zimbabwe, reflecting the final chapters of colonialism.

21. The area classification in table 2.1 and subsequent tables follows that found in the IMF's *International Financial Statistics*, hence the placement of some countries often classified as "Asian" in "Europe" and some normally North "African" countries in the "Middle East." The PRGF category of borrowers did not exist in 1975, much less in 1945. Although India is technically PRGF eligible, we classify it with the emerging-market countries.

22. Data on IMF credit outstanding, which reflect current programs as well as recently completed and in some cases suspended programs, provide a more informative picture of the pattern of the Fund's financial operations than the number or size of programs at particular dates. The data I have assembled, as best I can determine, capture all member countries that borrowed from the IMF during the 1975–2005 period, as well as prior to 1975, with the exception of Czechoslovakia/Czech Republic. Czechoslovakia rejoined the IMF in September 1990. Soon thereafter in March 1991 it received financial support from the IMF in the form of a 14-month program. Following the Velvet Revolution in 1993 that led to the creation of two countries—the Czech Republic and the Slovak Republic—the Czech Republic took on its share of the IMF credit outstanding to it, had a new program starting in March 1993, but

Table 2.1   IMF members, 2005

Region	Industrial countries (24)	Emerging-market countries (22)	Other developing countries (61)	Countries eligible to borrow from the PRGF (77)
Africa (53)	—	South Africa (1)	Algeria, Bahrain, Botswana, Equatorial Guinea, Gabon, Mauritius, Morocco, Namibia, Seychelles, Swaziland, Tunisia (11)	Angola, Benin, Burkina Faso, Burundi, Cameroon, Cape Verde, Central African Republic, Chad, Comoros, Democratic Republic of Congo, Republic of Congo, Côte d'Ivoire, Djibouti, Eritrea, Ethiopia, Gambia, Ghana, Guinea, Guinea-Bissau, Kenya, Kiribati, Lesotho, Liberia, Madagascar, Malawi, Mali, Mauritania, Mozambique, Niger, Nigeria, Rwanda, São Tomé and Principe, Senegal, Sierra Leone, Somalia, Sudan, Tanzania, Togo, Uganda, Zambia, Zimbabwe (41)
Asia (34)	Australia, Japan, New Zealand (3)	China, India, Indonesia, South Korea, Malaysia, Philippines, Singapore, Thailand (8)	Brunei Darussalam, Fiji, Marshall Islands, Micronesia, Palau (5)	Afghanistan, Bangladesh, Bhutan, Cambodia, Laos, Maldives, Mongolia, Myanmar, Nepal, Pakistan, Papua New Guinea, Samoa, Solomon Islands, Sri Lanka, Timor-Leste, Tonga, Vanuatu, Vietnam (18)
Europe (49)	Austria, Belgium, Denmark, Finland, France, Germany, Greece, Iceland, Ireland, Italy, Luxembourg, Netherlands, Norway, Portugal, San Marino, Spain, Sweden, Switzerland, United Kingdom (19)	Turkey, Russia, Hungary, Czech Republic, Poland (5)	Belarus, Bosnia and Herzegovina, Bulgaria, Croatia, Cyprus, Estonia, Kazakhstan, Latvia, Lithuania, Macedonia, Malta, Romania, Serbia and Montenegro, Slovak Republic, Slovenia, Turkmenistan, Ukraine (17)	Albania, Azerbaijan, Armenia, Georgia, Kyrgyz Republic, Moldova, Tajikistan, Uzbekistan (8)
Middle East (14)		Egypt (1)	Iran, Iraq, Israel, Jordan, Kuwait, Lebanon, Libya, Oman, Qatar, Saudi Arabia, Syria, United Arab Emirates (12)	Yemen (1)
Western Hemisphere (34)	Canada, United States (2)	Argentina, Brazil, Chile, Colombia, Ecuador, Mexico, Venezuela (7)	Antigua and Barbuda, Bahamas, Barbados, Belize, Costa Rica, Dominican Republic, El Salvador, Guatemala, Jamaica, Panama, Paraguay, Peru, St. Kitts and Nevis, Suriname, Trinidad and Tobago, Uruguay (16)	Bolivia, Dominica, Grenada, Guyana, Haiti, Honduras, Nicaragua, St. Lucia, St. Vincent and the Grenadines (9)

PRGF = Poverty Reduction and Growth Facility

Source: IMF Members' Quotas and Voting Power, and IMF Board of Governors, November 7, 2005, available at www.imf.org.

Table 2.2 Composition of IMF membership, 2005 and 1975

Classification of countries	Africa	Asia	Europe	Middle East	Western Hemisphere	Total
2005						
Industrial countries	0	3	19	0	2	24
Emerging-market countries[a]	1	8	5	1	7	22
Other developing countries	11	5	17	12	16	61
PRGF-eligible countries[b]	41	18	8	1	9	77
Total	53	34	49	14	34	184
1975						
Industrial countries	0	3	17	0	2	22
Emerging-market countries[a]	1	8	1	1	7	18
Other developing countries	9	1	4	12	12	38
PRGF-eligible countries[b]	31	10	0	2	6	49
Total	41	22	22	15	27	127

PRGF = Poverty Reduction and Growth Facility

a. Even though India is PRGF eligible, we classify it as an emerging-market economy because it is often treated as such by market participants.
b. Based on IMF categorization as of March 2005.

Source: IMF, *International Financial Statistics,* 2005 and 1975.

represented about 10 percent of the countries with credit outstanding from the IMF, in contrast with zero from 1990 until today. Over the entire period, emerging-market countries with credit outstanding fluctuated from 13 percent of the total number of borrowers in 1975 and 9 percent in 1980 to a high of 18 percent five years later and only 7 percent today. Current PRGF-eligible countries with IMF credit outstanding rose steadily from 58 percent of all borrowers in 1975 to 73 percent today. Finally, the share of other developing countries among all countries with IMF credit outstanding has fluctuated between 20 and 30 percent since 1980.

---

entirely repaid the IMF in 1994. Consequently it is not recorded as having had credit outstanding from the IMF in either 1990 or 1995. These data also do not cover countries that had only a precautionary SBA or EFF and did not draw upon those arrangements: Colombia, Nigeria, and Paraguay. Colombia and Paraguay had such programs in May 2005.

Table 2.3 Distribution of members with IMF credit outstanding, 1975–2005 (percent)

Category of country	1975	1980	1985	1990	1995	2000	2005[a]
Industrial countries	11	10	2	0	0	0	0
Emerging-market countries[b]	13	9	18	16	11	11	7
Western Hemisphere	4	1	6	7	5	4	4
Asia	6	5	8	6	2	4	2
Other	4	3	4	3	4	2	1
Other developing countries	17	20	20	22	30	22	20
PRGF-eligible countries[c]	58	61	60	62	59	67	73
Africa	34	39	37	41	37	40	44
Other	25	23	23	21	22	28	29
Total	100	100	100	100	100	100	100
Memorandum:							
Total number of countries with credit outstanding	53	80	87	86	98	91	85
Countries with credit outstanding as a percent of total members	42	57	58	56	55	50	46

PRGF = Poverty Reduction and Growth Facility

a. Data as of May 31, 2005.
b. Even though India is PRGF eligible, we classify it as an emerging-market economy because it is often treated as such by market participants.
c. Based on IMF categorization as of March 2005.

Note: Data capture all member countries that borrowed from the IMF during the 1975–2005 period, with the exception of Czechoslovakia/Czech Republic. This country was briefly indebted to the IMF between 1991 and 1994. Consequently, it was not picked up as having had credit outstanding to the IMF in either 1990 or 1995. See footnote 22 in the text for details.

Sources: IMF, *International Financial Statistics* (various years); IMF Annual Reports (various years).

Equally important to understanding the IMF's evolution as a lender is the distribution of the *amount* of IMF credit outstanding to different categories of members at five-year intervals during the 1975–2005 period. Table 2.4 provides some relevant data. With respect to categories of countries (top panel), in 1975 almost half of IMF credit outstanding was to industrial countries, but that rapidly diminished to zero by the late 1980s. In contrast, IMF credit to the group identified as emerging-market countries rose steadily from 27 percent in 1975 to 76 percent today.[23] As indi-

___

23. Contrary to the impression left by some official rhetoric in recent years about more limited lending to large borrowers, total IMF credit outstanding to emerging-market countries (the principal large borrowers) as of May 31, 2005, was SDR 42.2 billion compared with SDR 34.3 billion at the end of 2000.

Table 2.4   Distribution of IMF credit outstanding, 1975–2005 (percent)

Category of country/region	1975	1980	1985	1990	1995	2000	2005[a]
Industrial countries	48	12	2	0	0	0	0
Emerging-market countries[b]	27	35	60	60	63	70	76
Other developing countries	7	16	13	11	15	9	10
PRGF-eligible countries[c]	19	37	24	29	22	21	14
Total	100	100	100	100	100	100	100
Africa	8	26	22	25	17	13	9
Asia	28	38	30	15	12	38	15
Europe	49	20	10	4	27	34	28
Middle East	4	5	1	1	1	1	1
Western Hemisphere	11	11	37	55	43	14	47
Total	100	100	100	100	100	100	100
Memorandum:							
Total credit outstanding (in billions of SDR)	7.4	11.1	37.7	23.3	41.6	49.3	55.6
Percent of total quotas	25.1	17.6	40.0	25.6	28.6	23.4	26.0

PRGF = Poverty Reduction and Growth Facility
SDR = special drawing rights

a. Data as of May 31, 2005.
b. Even though India is PRGF eligible, we classify it as an emerging-market economy because it is often treated as such by market participants.
c. Based on IMF categorization as of March 2005.

Note: Data capture all member countries that borrowed from the IMF during the 1975–2005 period, with the exception of Czechoslovakia/Czech Republic. This country was briefly indebted to the IMF between 1991 and 1994. Consequently, it was not picked up as having had credit outstanding to the IMF in either 1990 or 1995. See footnote 22 in the text for more details.

Source: IMF, *International Financial Statistics* (various years).

cated in the second memorandum item in table 2.4, IMF credit outstanding as a percentage of total IMF quotas appears to have been remarkably stable at about 25 percent, with 1980 an outlier on the low side and 1985 on the high side. However, these ratios are affected somewhat by the timing of quota increases.

Interestingly, credit outstanding to PRGF-eligible countries reached its peak in 1980 at 37 percent of the total and is now only 14 percent. The decline during the past five years in part reflects the Heavily Indebted Poor Countries (HIPC) program of write-offs of debt to the IMF and other international financial institutions; but it is notable that by 1995, well before this phase of the HIPC program began, those countries accounted for only 22 percent of the total.

With respect to regions of the world (lower panel), the share of IMF credit outstanding to countries in the Western Hemisphere rose to a peak

Table 2.5 Proportion of countries within groups with credit outstanding, 1975–2005 (percent)

Category of country/region	1975	1980	1985	1990	1995	2000	2005[a]
Industrial countries	27	36	9	0	0	0	0
Emerging-market countries[b]	39	39	84	67	50	45	27
Other developing countries	24	40	40	42	51	33	28
PRGF-eligible countries[c]	63	82	80	80	76	80	81
Total (all IMF members)	**42**	**57**	**58**	**56**	**55**	**50**	**46**
Africa	44	77	74	79	77	75	74
Asia	55	64	70	57	35	39	32
Europe	36	41	22	12	50	44	35
Middle East	20	13	13	21	21	14	21
Western Hemisphere	44	55	71	68	58	44	44
Total (all IMF members)	**42**	**57**	**58**	**56**	**55**	**50**	**46**

PRGF = Poverty Reduction and Growth Facility

a. Data as of May 31, 2005.
b. Even though India is PRGF eligible, we classify it as an emerging-market economy because it is often treated as such by market participants.
c. Based on IMF categorization as of March 2005.

Note: Data capture all member countries that borrowed from the IMF during the 1975–2005 period, with the exception of Czechoslovakia/Czech Republic. This country was briefly indebted to the IMF between 1991 and 1994. Consequently, it was not picked up as having had credit outstanding to the IMF in either 1990 or 1995. See footnote 22 in the text for details.

Sources: IMF, *International Financial Statistics* (various years); IMF Annual Reports (various years).

in 1990, had declined sharply by 2000, but today amounts to almost half of the total because of large programs with Argentina, Brazil, and Uruguay. The share of credit outstanding to members in Asia has had two peaks of 38 percent in 1980 and 2000, but it has since declined back to 15 percent, where it was in 1990. The share of credit to European countries declined after 1975, rose again during the 1990s with special lending programs for new members from Eastern Europe and the former Soviet Union, and has recently declined. Finally, the share of credit to African countries moved steadily downward after 1980.

Table 2.5 provides a final summary of the pattern of IMF lending activity during the past 30 years. The data show for each year the number of countries in each category (top panel) or in each regional group (bottom panel) with credit outstanding from the Fund as a percentage of the (changing) total number of countries in each category or in each regional group. What is most striking is the remarkable stability (and slight decline since 1985) in the share of the total number of countries with IMF credit outstanding; that share rose by 16 percentage points between 1975 and 1985 and subsequently has declined by 12 percentage points. During the entire period, industrial countries have declined from 27 percent with credit outstanding in 1975 to zero since the late 1980s. The proportion of PRGF-eligible countries with credit outstanding rose after 1975 and has remained near 80 percent ever since. Emerging-market countries reached a peak in these terms in 1985, and their percentage has been on a downtrend subsequently. The peak for other developing countries was in 1995, reflecting borrowing by new members in Eastern Europe and the former Soviet Union.

Given these data on IMF credit outstanding by categories of countries, it is not surprising that a high proportion of African members of the IMF have had credit outstanding from the IMF since 1980. The proportions of Western Hemisphere countries and Asian countries with credit outstanding from the Fund have been declining since 1985. The European pattern reflects the IMF's high level of involvement with its new European members. Finally, a remarkable feature revealed by the data in the table is the consistent, low level of initial involvement by Middle Eastern countries with the IMF in terms of IMF credit outstanding to them.[24]

An interesting question is how will or should the data presented in tables 2.1 through 2.5 evolve going forward. The answer will depend on the extent of (1) volatility in global economic and financial conditions, (2) vulnerability of different categories or groups of countries to those fluctuations as well as the strength of their own policy regimes, and (3) willingness of the IMF to lend.

One can be hopeful for continued favorable global economic and financial conditions. However, neither the national nor the global business cycle has been outlawed, and global economic and financial conditions are unlikely to remain as benign as they have been during the past few years.

On vulnerability, a strong case can be made that several emerging-market and other developing countries have successfully implemented macroeconomic and microeconomic structural improvements that have reduced their vulnerability to external or internal shocks. Moreover, these two groups have substantially increased their holdings of international reserves. From 1994 to 2004, the 22 emerging-market countries listed in table 2.1 increased their combined holdings of foreign exchange reserves by more than 300 percent. The average increase was 384 percent.[25] These

---

24. Evidence on the lack of close involvement of members from the Middle East with the IMF is that as of August 31, 2005, (1) only 57 percent of those members have ever agreed to the publication of their Article IV consultation reports (compared with 88 percent for the IMF's membership as a whole) and (2) only 34 percent of those members have allowed publication of ROSC modules completed for these countries (compared with 74 percent for the total membership) although the average number of modules completed per Middle Eastern country (3.1) is close to the IMF average (3.6) (IMF 2005g, table 1).

25. Excluding China and Russia, which had the largest increases, the average increase was 234 percent. The average increase in foreign exchange reserves for the eight emerging-market economies in Asia was 450 percent, with the most dramatic increases in China (1,000 percent), South Korea (640 percent), and India (500 percent).

countries as a group increased their foreign exchange reserves from eight times their combined IMF quotas in 1994 to 24 times them in 2004. The other developing countries increased their reserves by more than 275 percent. The average was 308 percent.[26] These countries as a group increased their reserves from three times to nine times their quotas.

Thus, as reviewed extensively in chapter 3 of the BIS Annual Report (2005), many of these countries have put themselves in positions in which they have taken out a considerable amount of self-insurance against future global economic and financial disruption and the possible need to borrow from the IMF, although uncovered risks definitely remain.

The jury is still out on the third factor—the willingness of the IMF to lend. Certainly, many observers and a number of key members of the IMF believe that the IMF should substantially curtail the scale of its lending to emerging-market and other developing countries with normal, if not continuous, access to international capital markets. If these countries qualify for IMF loans, the size of those loans should be sharply restricted relative to their quotas. This view, if it prevails, could well lead to a further increase in self-insurance with respect to improved policies and further increases in international reserves.[27] The result might be a significant further reduction in IMF credit outstanding to countries other than the PRGF-eligible countries.

With respect to the PRGF-eligible countries, a substantial number of observers and a few members of the IMF have the view that IMF lending should be sharply curtailed or should be shifted to the World Bank while IMF programs of technical assistance and policy advice in the form of nonborrowing programs should continue.

In addition to these trends and attitudes, a number of East European countries are now under the political, economic, and one would presume financial umbrella of the European Union. If they are in need of financial assistance during the next decade, they will not turn first to the IMF. Many Asian countries are strongly averse to borrowing from the IMF given their experience in the late 1990s and are actively involved in transforming the

---

26. These data are for only 48 of the 61 "other developing countries" listed in table 2.1 because data are not available on the foreign exchange reserves of the other 13 countries in 1994 and/or 2004.

27. Eduardo Borensztein (2004) presents a number of indicators of potential demands for IMF resources over the next 20 to 50 years. He argues that the heavy borrowers from the Fund today, in terms of total amounts borrowed, are the middle-income countries. He further argues that the share of those countries in the total membership of the IMF should rise over this period, in particular during the next 20 years. Finally, he calculates that if China and India qualified for a package of IMF financial assistance as large as that received by Mexico in 1995 (6.3 percent of GDP) at the point where their estimated levels of income were similar (in 2018 and 2032 respectively), the financial demands on the IMF would dwarf the Fund's likely resources.

Chiang Mai Initiative into an Asian Monetary Fund—a more kindly and understanding version of the Washington institution (Henning 2002).[28]

Thus, it is possible to imagine an IMF in the future that only occasionally embarks on new lending programs. Those programs may be limited to a few emerging-market and developing economies in Latin America that have not built up large reserve cushions. At most, the Fund will become a development institution doing very little lending. At worst, it might wither away or be closed down as some observers have recommended.[29]

On the other hand, it is too easy to say that the IMF will continue to exist but that it will become an institution that lends to an increasingly limited group of countries, with the membership of the institution sharply differentiated between lenders and borrowers. Industrial countries have not borrowed from the IMF for decades, and it is difficult to imagine that they will ever again, but Boughton (2005) reminds us that the revolving character of the IMF continues to be relevant to understanding its role. He reports that from 1980 to 2004, 44 countries have moved from a situation of being net lenders to the Fund to finance IMF lending operations to becoming net borrowers from the Fund and back again to becoming net lenders. He also reports that as of 2004, 58 of the 129 countries that he classifies as developing countries—excluding industrial countries and market borrowers—had positive net financial positions in the IMF.[30] Of these, 15 were net creditors to the Fund.[31]

IMF Reform Efforts

Whither the IMF? How should it be reformed? There has been no dearth of ideas. Ten years ago, the Bretton Woods Commission (1994) emphasized in

---

28. Evidence of the disaffection of Asian developing countries from the IMF is that as of August 31, 2005, (1) only 76 percent of them have ever allowed their Article IV reports to be published (compared with the IMF average of 88 percent), (2) only 5 of the 29 countries—17 percent—have had FSAPs (compared with the IMF average of 50 percent), and (3) only 45 percent have had ROSC modules completed (compared with 66 percent for the IMF as a whole). The average number of ROSC modules is 1.8 per Asian country (IMF average 3.6), and only 51 percent of completed modules for Asian countries have been published (IMF average 74 percent) (IMF 2005g, table 1).

29. Among those who have advocated closing down the IMF are Allan Meltzer ("Why It Is Time to Close Down the IMF," *Financial Times,* June 16, 1995) because of the moral hazard he believes is associated with IMF lending; George Shultz, William Simon, and Walter Wriston ("Who Needs the IMF?" *Wall Street Journal,* February 3, 1998) on the grounds that the IMF is no longer needed; and Milton Friedman (2004), arguing that the Fund (and the Bank) have done substantially more harm than good.

30. Their reserve tranche positions, consisting of reserve assets they have paid into the IMF, were positive.

31. Their reserve tranche positions were larger than the reserve assets they have paid into the IMF because they have lent their currencies through the IMF to other countries.

its conclusions that the IMF should play a larger role in the international monetary system, seeking greater exchange rate stability and better coordination of economic policies. The Commission also advocated concentration on sound macroeconomic policies in IMF lending programs and its reduced duplication of the functions of the World Bank. Finally, it called for improved governance, including adjustment of quota shares in line with "the changed realities of relative economic importance in world trade, capital flows, and GNP," increased openness, and explaining its mission better.

In the late 1990s, in the wake of, first, the Mexican crisis and, later, the East Asian financial crises, the Russian default, and the Brazilian crises, public and private groups issued a flurry of reports and proposals for IMF reform. Barry Eichengreen (1999) provides a nice summary of the debate on reform of the international financial architecture as of the late 1990s along with some proposals of his own. Robert Rubin and Jacob Weisberg (2003) provide an insider's view of the initial evolution of the debate on the international financial architecture.[32]

A report of a study group sponsored by the Council on Foreign Relations (1999) included seven priority items for IMF reform:

- The IMF should lend on more favorable terms to countries that take effective steps to reduce their crisis vulnerability.

- Emerging-market countries with fragile financial systems should discourage short-term capital inflows.

- The private sector should promote fair burden sharing in workout situations, including the adoption of collective action clauses; and IMF lending to countries in arrears to the private sector should be subject to tight conditions on "good faith" negotiations with those creditors.

- Emerging-market countries should not adopt exchange rate regimes with pegged rates.

- The IMF should abandon large rescue packages and adhere to its normal lending limits.

- Both the IMF and World Bank should focus on their core responsibilities and limit operations in the other institution's domain.

- A global conference should meet and agree to priorities and timetables to strengthen national financial systems.

Note that six of these seven prescriptions, and implicitly a seventh (the sixth bullet item), relate almost exclusively to the IMF's role vis-à-vis emerging-market economies.

---

32. "International financial architecture" was the lofty phrase that Secretary of the Treasury Rubin first used in a 1995 speech that sought to set out US thinking on the subject of reform of the IMF and the international financial system.

One of the most prominent and influential reports with regard to Washington opinion was that of the congressionally chartered International Financial Institutions Advisory Commission (IFIAC 2000), also known as the Meltzer Commission. The central set of its recommendations focused on IMF lending in crisis situations, which the IFIAC agreed should continue. However, the majority view was that after a transition period such lending should be limited only to countries that had prequalified for such lending on the basis of a short list of criteria. Moreover, that lending should be short-term lending at a penalty interest rate. The IFIAC also recommended closing the PRGF, but that recommendation was understood to encompass its possible transfer to the World Bank.[33]

In response to some of the reports and recommendations that were appearing at the time, and in part to anticipate the recommendations of the IFIAC, Secretary of the Treasury Lawrence Summers on December 14, 1999, delivered a speech entitled "The Right Kind of IMF for a Stable Global Financial System" at the London School of Business. He made six basic points and proposals for the IMF:

- promote the flow of better information to markets;

- focus on financial vulnerabilities as well as macroeconomic vulnerabilities;

- be selective in providing its financial support, inter alia, because "[t]he IMF cannot expect its financial capacity to grow in parallel with the growth of private-sector financial flows;"

- improve engagement with the private sector on capital market issues by setting up a capital markets advisory group and rationalizing its approach to private-sector involvement in the management of financial crises;

- refocus support of growth and poverty reduction in the low-income countries; and

- reform institutionally in terms of transparency and openness and also in its governance structure.

On the final point, Summers said the IMF "should move over time toward a governing structure that is more representative and a relative allocation of quotas that reflects changes under way in the world economy—so that each country's standing and voice is more consistent with their relative economic and financial strength."

---

33. John Williamson (2001) summarizes the major reports issued after the first round of debates along with some ideas of his own. See also the review of reform proposals in Goldstein (2003).

Substantial movement, many observers would say progress, has been made on most of the areas highlighted by Summers. Where there has not been movement, for example, in the area of IMF governance, the issues are still very much alive.

US Acting Under Secretary Quarles (2005) summarized the progress that has been made in recent years on IMF reform, understandably emphasizing a break with the past more than the record supports. He said that limits and criteria for IMF lending have been clarified. He noted that the IMF is now focused more directly on its core macroeconomic areas of expertise, including financial sectors. He said that more attention is being given to short-term financing. He highlighted the increase in IMF transparency and work on codes and standards for the financial system. He noted the progress on crisis management with many countries embracing the use of collective action clauses (CACs) in their international borrowing instruments.[34]

Looking forward, Quarles identified the importance of the IMF's strengthening surveillance and crisis prevention, promoting strong policies without lending (nonborrowing programs), and effectively supporting low-income countries. He also noted that Secretary Snow beginning in October 2004 had "emphasized that change is needed to address the growing disparity between the IMF's governance structure and the realities of the world economy."

Some observers have other lists of priorities. James Boughton (2004) highlights four key reforms:

- strengthening surveillance and early warning systems;

- designing lending programs to restore market access and growth;

- providing appropriate direction of policy advice and financial support for low-income countries; and

- improving the equity and effectiveness of IMF governance.

Timothy Lane (2005) identifies five key open issues for the IMF:

- consensus on the IMF's role in the prevention and management of crises in emerging-market economies;

- the scope of IMF conditionality;

- the seriousness of the phenomenon of prolonged use of IMF resources (borrowings outstanding) and what to do about it;

---

34. Immediately following the 1995 Mexican crisis, collective action clauses were proposed by informed observers (Eichengreen and Portes 1995), endorsed by the official sector (G-10 1996), but resisted by the private financial sector. This reform took almost 10 years and a great deal of dedicated analysis and persuasion to bring to fruition.

- the IMF's involvement with low-income countries; and

- governance issues.

Goldstein (2005a) puts forward a list with a somewhat different focus and orientation:

- stronger injunctions against exchange rate manipulation;

- better identification and control of currency mismatches in emerging-market countries;

- even greater emphasis on debt sustainability in IMF surveillance;

- improving the quality of compliance evaluations with international standards and codes;

- giving greater weight to early warnings of currency, banking, and debt crises; and

- limiting lending in "exceptional access" cases to cases that are truly exceptional.

Boughton, Lane, and Goldstein recommend rather disparate approaches to IMF reform. As indicated earlier, some observers favor narrowing the IMF's focus, for example, to lending to the developing countries other than those with normal market access, perhaps on a precommitted basis, or to concentrating only on financial-sector issues in those countries. Alternatively, the IMF's focus might be narrowed principally to emerging-market countries and the sustainability of their debts and their vulnerability to disruption.

Meanwhile, the IMF itself embarked in 2005 on a medium-term strategic review (MTSR) with the aim of developing a medium-term strategy.[35] The review is internal, but it is under the guidance of the Executive Board and ultimately the IMFC. On the basis of published reports (Managing Director de Rato's address at the joint IMF/Bundesbank symposium on June 8, 2005; IMF 2005j; IMF 2005f), the review was expected to cover five broad topics:

- the effectiveness and impact of surveillance;

- the IMF's analysis of financial sectors and international capital markets;

- the IMF's lending activities;

- the Fund's role in low-income countries; and

---

35. This exercise was originally a G-7 initiative.

- various aspects of IMF governance, including internal management issues and voice and participation in the institution by a broader range of countries.

The IMF issued Managing Director de Rato's Report on the Fund's Medium-Term Strategy on September 15, 2005; see chapter 1.

One topic that has been missing from most recent agendas for IMF reform, with the exception of the report of the Bretton Woods Commission more than a decade ago, is the IMF's role in the management of the international monetary and financial system, in particular with regard to exchange rate misalignments and global economic imbalances.[36] At the April 2005 IMFC, representatives of the G-7 countries and the European Union (finance ministers Breton, Brown, Eichel, Goodale, Junker, Siniscalco, Snow, and Tanigaki) paid lip service to the objective of achieving greater macroeconomic and financial stability insofar as their own macroeconomic policies were concerned. However, in their comments on the IMF's strategic direction, none articulated a role for the IMF in this area. Instead, they implicitly presented a view that the IMF's primary role should be restricted to nonindustrial countries, preferably the non-emerging-market countries. The logical inference is that the IMF should become just another development institution. The next chapter critically examines the role of the IMF in the international monetary system.

---

36. Most observers use the terms "international monetary system" and "international financial system" interchangeably. My preference is to reserve the first term for the conventions, rules, and structures associated with official actions and policies and to reserve the second term for the broader set of conventions, rules, and structures that involve private-sector participants as well, with the second encompassing the first. However, in this policy analysis I, too, use the terms interchangeably.

Role in the International Monetary System

Mervyn King, in his remarks on the international monetary system at a conference, "Advancing Enterprise 2005," on February 4, 2005, summarized succinctly the view that the IMF should have a major role in addressing the proper functioning of the international monetary system:

> The international monetary system should be seen not as a series of bilateral relationships, but as a multilateral arrangement, albeit one where a small number [larger than the G-7] of key players can usefully communicate with each other. I think we need to rethink the role of the IMF in the international monetary system. . . . I am not convinced that the future of the Fund is primarily as an occasional international lender of last resort for middle-income countries suffering financial crises.

King's remarks suggest an IMF role that is broad and should contribute more than it does today to substantial cooperation, if not coordination, on national policies affecting the international economy and financial system. Others are highly skeptical about international macroeconomic policy coordination and by implication the role of any international organization in fostering such coordination. For example, Horst Siebert (2005) at a conference on the IMF stated, "The best that governments can do is to follow an atmospheric coordination, i.e., exchanging information on the situation and the paradigm to be used."

This chapter examines the IMF's role (1) in surveillance, (2) with regard to exchange rates and policies, (3) in capital account and financial-sector issues, and (4) with respect to regional arrangements. All four aspects are central to an effective role of the IMF in the international monetary system. In general, if the IMF is to play these roles effectively, it has to be more of an umpire and not just an adviser and sometime lender.

Surveillance

It is widely agreed that surveillance and the associated process of policy coordination and cooperation are central roles of the IMF. Effective surveillance can help to solve the type of coordination problems that undermined the health of the global economy in the 1930s and led to the founding of the IMF at the end of World War II. Under the Bretton Woods system, coordination was forced through the fixed exchange rate system (gold exchange standard). With the forced abandonment of that system in the 1970s, surveillance remains an instrument to deal with imbalances in the global economic and financial system.

The disagreement today is how surveillance fits into the IMF's overall mission and whether surveillance has anything to do with the health of the international monetary system. Thus, the IMFC (2005) concluded:

> Surveillance is a central task of the IMF and determined efforts are required to enhance its effectiveness and impact, building on the conclusions of the Biennial Review of Surveillance. Surveillance should become more focused and selective in analyzing issues, in an evenhanded way across the membership. Regional and global surveillance should play an increasingly important role, and be better integrated with bilateral surveillance.

The IMFC's conclusions, although they mention the important role of regional and global surveillance that presumably has something to do with the functioning of the international monetary system, do not provide much guidance for what the IMF should be doing. The conclusions do point to the three levels of surveillance: national, regional, and multilateral. It is principally in its multilateral surveillance role that the IMF becomes concerned with the functioning of the international monetary system. To the extent that the policies and performances of individual countries or groups of countries affect the health and smooth functioning of the system, national and regional surveillance are also relevant.

The relevant questions with respect to the IMF and the international monetary system include: What is the scope of such surveillance and what variables and policies should it cover? Should the IMF more aggressively engage with countries on their exchange rate policies? How can the IMF be made more effective in altering exchange rate and other policies? Should the IMF have a larger role to play in policy coordination? How can the IMF perform its current role better? Or should it have a different role?

Currently many of the concerns and criticisms of the role of the IMF in the international monetary system are connected with the perception that global economic imbalances are a threat to international economic and financial stability and the IMF should be doing more about them. Of course, the IMF has hardly been silent on these issues, featuring them in successive reports on the *World Economic Outlook* and issuing special analyses of the general issue or on aspects of it, such as US fiscal policy. Managing Director de Rato devoted more than half of his remarks at the IESE Business School, University of Navarra, Madrid, on June 10, 2005, to the issue of global imbalances.

Global imbalances and the policies that support their continuation largely, but not entirely, involve the major economies: the United States, the euro area, and Japan. However, many informed and sympathetic observers despair about making any progress in this area. For example, Timothy Geithner commented before the Bretton Woods Committee on June 10, 2004, that the Fund "will never be decisive . . . in persuading the G-3 to avoid policies that create the risk of abrupt changes in financial market conditions or exchange rates."

The basic problem, as described by David Peretz (2005) and many others, is that the IMF lacks leverage over the policies of countries that do not need, and especially those that never anticipate having a need, to borrow from the Fund. In addition, these countries either do not agree that their policies risk adverse global effects or, if they agree, they are unable for domestic political reasons to do anything to affect their policies.

Even for those observers who agree there is a need, effective remedies are not easy to design. Some candidates for remedies include the following:

- *Increase transparency.* This is a general prescription for many of the problems of the international financial system, but it applies with some vigor to global surveillance. José De Gregorio et al. (1999) advocate increased transparency with regard to the IMF's internal operations along with increased independence for the Executive Board and the staff.[1] Their focus is principally with regard to IMF relations with emerging-market countries, but one could argue those recommendations also should be relevant to the larger economies that potentially affect the health of the international monetary system. Barry Eichengreen (2004) repeats his recommendation that all IMF surveillance documents should be released to the public, rather than leaving discretion with each country.

- *Increase candor.* The IMF (management and staff) has become more candid in recent years in its pronouncements on risks to the international financial system and the links between those risks and the policies of the major economies. However, both Michel Camdessus and Jacques de Larosière (Camdessus, de Larosière, and Köhler 2004) point to the need for G-7 countries to listen more carefully to what the IMF is saying and for greater focus on systemic interactions in the process of multilateral surveillance. Increased candor probably should be

---

1. Prompt publication of detailed minutes of Executive Board meetings, decisions through voting, and voting records is one example.

coupled with increased IMF humility. When the IMF staff or management predicts a disaster and the disaster does not occur, there should be an explanation of why—changes in circumstances or wrong policy prescriptions.

- *Specify remedies.* IMF reports on countries that are systemically significant often suggest appropriate changes in policies. IMF reports on the risks facing the global economy do the same. However, those suggestions are general in nature—tighten fiscal policy, avoid financial bubbles, intensify structural adjustment. The IMF might go several steps further and specify as precisely as possible the size if not the content of the policy adjustments it would require if the policy excesses of the countries involved were to lead to a need to borrow from the IMF. This approach could be applied even in cases where such an eventuality was highly unlikely. The more specific the IMF was in its advice, the more specific the country would have to be in rejecting that advice.

- *Issue ratings.* It has been proposed, and to date rejected, that the IMF issue ratings of countries. Again, this proposal normally is advanced in the context of IMF surveillance of countries that might reasonably be expected to borrow from the IMF, but why should there not be a rating system that applies to countries whose policies have systemic significance?

- *Develop scorecards.* Timothy Geithner, in his remarks before the Bretton Woods Committee, endorsed for emerging-market countries "a process with more frequent, publicized [IMF] staff assessments of performance against a medium-term framework designed by a member country." That approach could be extended to all systemically important countries, including important industrial countries.

- *Change the paradigm.* Multilateral surveillance and the associated surveillance of the systemically important members of the IMF are process driven. Even when multilateral surveillance is subjected to independent evaluation, that evaluation is likely to be process oriented. The IMF's Independent Evaluation Office is currently evaluating IMF multilateral surveillance. The draft issues paper (IMF-IEO 2005d, 11) identifies two objectives: "(i) contributing to transparency by showing how multilateral surveillance works in practice and (ii) identifying areas, *if any*, where improvement can be made to make multilateral surveillance more effective" (emphasis added). This is not a very ambitious work program.

What may be needed is to change the paradigm of IMF surveillance. The Fund might start from the needs and objectives of the international monetary system, work back from that assessment to what the assessment implies about the policies of the systemically important countries, and use the framework to evaluate actual policies. A reasonable, but not the only, place to start this evaluation might be exchange rates. A widespread view is that (1) excessive exchange rate stability or (2) excessive swings (or excessive instability) in exchange rates among the major currencies contribute to imbalances that threaten global prosperity. A framework of this type is John Williamson's (1985) target zone proposal that he has articulated and advocated for many years in a number of different forms and formats; see also Williamson (2000) and Williamson's chapter 6 in the forthcoming conference volume. An alternative framework might start from an evaluation of global saving and investment. This starting point would be likely to produce norms similar to those associated with Williamson's target zones or reference rates.

If the IMF were to adopt a new paradigm to use in conducting its multilateral surveillance, the first step would need to be the development of a consensus on that paradigm. The development of such a consensus need not initially involve the major countries. A substantial subset of other members of the IMF, if they were sufficiently likeminded, could initiate the debate. The IMF management and staff also could instigate it.

Given the central role of surveillance as one of the Fund's principal tools and how surveillance relates not only to global economic and financial stability but also to the design and desirability of individual lending arrangements, a number of officials and observers (Brown 2005 and Ubide 2005, to name two) have suggested that the surveillance function become fully independent of the IMF's lending programs and other programs, including for the large countries and presumably with respect to regional and global surveillance.[2] The IMF as an institution might consist of two subsidiaries, the surveillance subsidiary and the program subsidiary, both reporting to the management (managing director and deputy managing directors) and the Executive Board. Alternatively, the IMF could be split into two separate institutions. This would be an expensive solution in terms of staff resources and could sow confusion if the two bodies reached different conclusions, which would be reasonable because most important cases come down to a matter of judgment, not analysis.[3] Goldstein (2005a) would address the surveillance of emerging-market economies by more intense concentration on early-warning surveillance, compared with routine Article IV surveillance.

---

2. US Treasury Secretary Snow (2004) told the IMFC that the United States is open to the idea.

3. One argument that motivates advocates of separating the lending and surveillance functions of the IMF is the perception that Fund staff and management have a bias toward lending to help countries and that this bias clouds their perspective on the advisability of doing so. The counterargument is that, if this is a correct depiction, it reflects a management failure instead of a structural failure.

An unfortunate side effect of the emphasis on the link between the quality of IMF surveillance and the quality of IMF lending programs that is made by some critics has been that the role of IMF surveillance with respect to global economic and financial stability is often viewed as a second-class activity. Moreover, many critics and observers fail to make the distinction between IMF surveillance before a country has a program—for example, with Thailand and Korea in 1996–97—and IMF surveillance after a country has some type of formal program—for example, with Argentina from the start of the 1990s through 2001.[4]

Exchange Rates and Policies

Exchange rates and exchange rate policies are an important subtopic in surveillance and the associated role of the IMF in the international monetary system. The vagaries of floating exchange rates have produced much handwringing from some prominent people, including, for example, Paul Volcker in his remarks before the Institute of International Finance in Washington on October 10, 1998:

> We still hear the siren song that somehow floating exchange rates will solve the problem. That seems to me a strange and sad refrain. The wide swings in the exchange rate of the world's two largest economies, Japan and the US, has been a critically important factor contributing to the instability of East Asia generally. How can there be a 'correct' rate, fixed or floating, for Thailand or Indonesia or the Philippines when the exchange rates of their major trading partners are diverging sharply? How can it be rational for some Asian countries to be advised to float their currencies while others are urged to stand firm in fixing their exchange rates, even while their competitive positions are deteriorating?

More recently, two former IMF managing directors have commented on the issue. In 2004, Michel Camdessus (Camdessus, de Larosière, and Köhler 2004) wrote:

> I still cannot reconcile myself to a degree of instability of exchange rates—every 10 years or so we observe swings of up to 50 percent in the exchange rates of the major reserve currencies—that is so costly for the entire system, so disruptive for vulnerable countries, and acceptable only to (if not welcomed by) those whose job it is to provide profitable cover against those fluctuations.

Jacques de Larosière (also in Camdessus, de Larosière, and Köhler 2004) came from a somewhat different perspective:

> I also believe the international monetary system is slipping into a semifixed à la carte system where some countries choose their exchange rate peg (often undervalued) to take the best advantage of their export capacities. The question is what should the IMF do about this situation?

---

4. Chapter 5 on IMF lending facilities touches upon the related issue of the link between IMF surveillance and a possible insurance facility in the IMF.

Morris Goldstein (2005a) has an answer to de Larosière's question. The IMF can and should pursue much more aggressively countries that engage in "currency manipulation" by pegging their exchange rates for extended periods of time at undervalued levels while piling up foreign exchange reserves and frustrating the international adjustment process. C. Fred Bergsten (testimony before the Subcommittee on International Trade and Finance of the US Senate Committee on Banking, Housing and Urban Affairs on June 7, 2005) echoes his colleague.

Managing Director de Rato in his report to the IMFC (IMF 2005f) called for a "deeper treatment of exchange rate issues" and noted that the Executive Board had held a seminar on operational aspects of moving toward greater exchange rate flexibility. However, the staff paper prepared for that discussion (IMF 2004a) was decidedly cool to regimes of floating exchange rates. It stressed that four ingredients are needed successfully to make the transition: (1) deep and liquid foreign exchange markets, (2) a coherent intervention policy, (3) an appropriate alternative nominal anchor such as inflation targeting, and (4) adequate systems to review and manage public- and private-sector exchange risks. If those are the tests for success with a flexible exchange rate regime, few countries with floating exchange rates are successful practitioners because most of them would fail one or more of those tests. This is not helpful IMF staff guidance.

It is not surprising that the IMF staff was so timid in its paper because the Executive Board for which it works and many national authorities for whom the executive directors work are deeply divided on these issues. The report of the executive directors' discussion (IMF 2004d) as well as ample other evidence imply that many policymakers are far from convinced that exchange rate flexibility is ever desirable. Adding more cautions to those advanced by the staff, for example, the executive directors

- voiced the familiar refrain that no single exchange rate regime is appropriate for all countries in all circumstances, without adding the qualification that it can be very costly to change regimes;

- called for more work on moving toward greater exchange rate stability, for example by joining regional exchange rate arrangements; and

- stressed the need to develop a global monitoring system for hedge funds if floating is to be successful, implying incorrectly that hedge funds are the most important source of speculation and exchange rate volatility in the international financial system.[5]

---

5. The Independent Evaluation Office of the IMF will be conducting a review of the IMF's advice on exchange rate policy (IMF-IEO 2005c). The review of IMF surveillance over exchange rate policies will touch on two sets of issues: (1) members' choices of exchange rate regimes and (2) the level of exchange rates in terms of competitiveness, exchange rate sustainability, and exchange rate manipulation. The focus will be the post-1998 period. From the perspective of the international monetary system, the second set of issues, in particular exchange rate manipulation, is most relevant.

If further evidence is needed to buttress the view that the IMF institutionally does not think consistently and coherently about exchange rates and exchange rate policies, consider two IMF reports on East Asian exchange rate arrangements that were completed in the fourth quarter of 2004. In the concluding statement of the Article IV mission to Korea (IMF 2004f) the staff "strongly supports the official policy of allowing the won's external value to be determined in the market, with intervention limited to smoothing operations." However, it was only shortly after this statement was released on October 28 that the Korean authorities scaled back their massive intervention operations and allowed the won to appreciate sharply over the balance of the year. The IMF staff praised a nonpolicy!

In contrast, in the documents associated with the Article IV consultation with Hong Kong conducted at essentially the same time (IMF 2005e), the staff assessment was that the authorities' "response to appreciation pressures over the past year has enhanced the resilience of the LERS [linked exchange rate system, i.e., peg to the US dollar]. The LERS remains robust and the staff continues to support the authorities' commitment to it."[6] In February 2005, the Executive Board (IMF 2005e) echoed the staff view: "They reiterated their support for the authorities' commitment to the LERS." One might reasonably ask how and why a hard peg between the Hong Kong dollar and the US dollar makes any economic sense; the two countries certainly are not an optimum currency area. Wouldn't a peg to the Chinese yuan make more sense over the long term? Doesn't the Hong Kong dollar's peg to the US dollar militate against an early, substantial adjustment of the Chinese yuan against the US dollar? One would hope that the IMF staff and Executive Board discussed the issue of the long-term viability of the Hong Kong dollar's peg and also the short-term what-if issue for Hong Kong of a substantial revaluation of the Chinese yuan. However, such discussions are not hinted at in the public documents. Their absence illustrates the tension between candor and transparency in IMF surveillance.[7]

Capital Accounts and Financial Sectors

IMF surveillance in practice also extends to members' capital accounts, including the size and composition of their external debts and the potential

---

6. The LERS at the time was asymmetric in the sense that it was softer on the upside. Subsequently, the regime has been hardened and has become symmetric.

7. A third example is Malaysia (IMF 2005a). The IMF staff concluded that in September 2004 the ringgit was undervalued by 3 to 5 percent in real effective terms, clearly an underestimate in the context of the prevailing global imbalances. In contrast, in the case of China the IMF staff has not even gone so far as to say that the yuan is undervalued. However, it was only the executive directors (most of them), not the staff, that called for IMF engagement with the Malaysian authorities about their policy alternatives with a view toward moving toward greater (than zero, bilateral) exchange rate flexibility.

for capital account crises. These crises, in turn, are often closely linked to financial-sector development and stability, an area in which the IMF has been assigned a major surveillance role along with the World Bank. In addition, capital controls are a major ingredient supporting exchange rate policies and the manipulation of exchange rates to present effective balance of payments adjustment. From a global perspective, all aspects are integral to the IMF's role in the international monetary and financial system.

As noted in chapter 2, IMF work on the financial-sector and capital account issues is not fully grounded in the Articles of Agreement. Possibly for that reason as well as others, the IMF's analysis of these issues is widely regarded as not satisfactory. Although the IMF Executive Board (IMF 2005c) commended the IMF staff on the "continuing success" of the FSAP, it is well known that many observers think the program has serious shortcomings. One point of controversy is that publication of the resulting ROSC modules is voluntary.[8] A second is that a major, systemically important country—the United States—has not had an FSAP.[9] Moreover, until 2002 Japan successfully resisted an FSAP review of its ailing financial system. For more than a decade previously, the Japanese financial system was widely seen as a threat to Japanese economic and financial stability as well as to global economic prosperity if not financial stability. Many would argue that this episode clearly indicates a weakness of the IMF in dealing with threats to the stability of the international monetary and financial system that originated in the malfunctioning financial sector of a major economy.

The IMF Independent Evaluation Office in 2005 conducted a review of the FSAP, including its links with Article IV surveillance as well as the design and implementation of the FSAP. As noted in chapter 2, the managing director assembled the McDonough Working Group to provide an assessment of the IMF's work on the financial system and capital markets.

Aside from the issue of authority, three basic issues are involved in the dissatisfaction with the IMF's work on capital account and financial-sector issues. First, the culture and work of the IMF is dominated by macroeconomists with little training or interest in financial-sector issues, and that emphasis carries over into the work of the area departments, which are ill equipped to analyze, or are uninterested in, financial-sector and capital market issues, reflecting either understaffing or staff with the wrong skills. Second, substantial IMF staff resources are devoted to the treatment of these issues, but the institutional payoffs are not associated with good analyses of particular problems. Instead, the major rewards are

---

8. The 68 percent of the member countries with completed ROSC modules have allowed a total of 74 percent of the results to be published (IMF 2005g, table 1).

9. The only other G-7 country that had not had an FSAP is Italy, which is currently undergoing a review. The only other non-G-7 G-10 country that had not had an FSAP is Belgium, which is also currently undergoing a review.

forthcoming for provocative overall assessments that are provided to the Executive Board and the general public. Third, when it comes to country surveillance in these areas, not only is it not well integrated with other aspects of surveillance but also it is, if anything, too comprehensive and lacking in prioritization.

On the broader but related issue of capital account policies, it is well known that the membership of the IMF debated during 1996–97 whether the IMF Articles of Agreement should be amended to (1) update and clarify the role of the IMF with respect to capital account transactions, (2) establish capital account liberalization as an objective for IMF members, and (3) establish the IMF's jurisdiction with respect to capital account matters.[10]

This initiative foundered on the fallout from the East Asian financial crises. Many commentators who should know better, including in the financial press, demonized the G-7 and the management of the IMF for this initiative. The facts are quite different. Stanley Fischer (1998) summarizes the case quite well:

> The increasing importance of international capital flows is a fact that needs to be better recognized in the laws and agreements that help bring order to the international economy and to the process by which individual countries liberalize their capital accounts. The proposed amendment to the IMF's Articles of Agreement will serve this purpose and the international community as well.

The statement attached to the September 21 communiqué of the Interim Committee (1997) issued in Hong Kong is quite balanced and circumscribed. It speaks of the growing importance of private capital movements and the necessity of ensuring the orderly liberalization of capital flows. It states that the IMF is uniquely placed to assist this process and asserts the committee's view that the Fund's new mandate in this area should be "bold in its vision, but cautious in its implementation." The Executive Board in its work on the proposed amendment was called on to make liberalization of capital movements one of the purposes of the Fund and to extend the Fund's jurisdiction over the liberalization process, but to do so with safeguards, transitional arrangements, flexible approval processes, and in recognition that in the new world of liberalized capital movements "there could be a large need for financing from the Fund and other sources." As noted, the Executive Board did not complete its work.

---

10. Capital account liberalization covers two broad areas: (1) cross-border access via direct investment and the ability to provide services by institutions that operate in the financial sector and (2) capital account flows or financial transactions. The first area is within the jurisdiction of the World Trade Organization (WTO). In the 1990s, the concern of some was that in the absence of a clear definition of the jurisdiction of the IMF over the second area, the WTO would further expand its mandate to cover this area as well. On the other hand, the Fund's authority over current account transactions pertains to payments (exchange restrictions), not the substance of those transactions—tariffs and quotas. The analogous distinction with respect to the capital account is more difficult to make.

Part of the controversy that emerged in the wake of the East Asian financial crises, the Brazilian crises, the Russian crisis, Turkey's crisis, and the Argentina debacle concerned not the aborted effort to amend the IMF Articles of Agreement with respect to capital account liberalization but the extent to which the Fund had been pushing capital account liberalization willy-nilly. The report of the IMF-IEO (2005a) did not confirm this accusation. It finds no evidence that the IMF as an institution used its leverage to push countries to move faster than they were willing to go in liberalizing their capital account transactions. Individual Fund staff, however, did in general encourage those countries that wanted to do so to move ahead without paying sufficient attention to the risks involved, the proper sequencing of the liberalization, and the interaction with domestic financial-sector development.

This lack of attention to sequencing and financial-sector development was caused in part by the absence of an official IMF position on capital account liberalization that allowed individual staff members the latitude to espouse their own disparate views when it came to advising members on these issues. The IMF-IEO report (2005a) recommends increased clarity on these matters and greater attention to supply-side aspects of international capital flows involving principally the industrial countries and efforts, for example, to limit herd behavior on the part of investors.[11]

Where is the IMF likely to go with the issue of the IMF's role in capital account liberalization? Peretz (2005) advocates revisiting the consensus of 1996–97 and reviving the idea of an amendment to the IMF Articles of Agreement on this topic.[12]

Jack Boorman, in remarks to an Institute of International Finance Seminar in London on November 17, 2004, also advocated revisiting this issue on jurisdiction grounds vis-à-vis the WTO. He also sees continuing potential for pressure on IMF resources from poorly designed and implemented liberalization programs. However, he cautions that first the IMF and its membership would need to clear the air on several issues:

- What was the IMF advising member countries with regard to capital account liberalization in the early and mid-1990s? The IMF-IEO appears to have dealt with this issue, although critics, being critics, no doubt will not be satisfied.

- The IMF needs to integrate into its regular operations the past decade's lessons with respect to capital account liberalization. This process seems to be under way but far from complete to the general satisfaction of most members.

---

11. Williamson (2005) addresses many of these issues in more detail than does the IMF-IEO report, and various IMF *Global Financial Stability Reports* have emphasized these issues.

12. Peretz's position is not altogether surprising, as he was a British official at the IMF in the 1990s and the UK government was a principal advocate for change at that time.

- The motivation of the amendment to the Articles of Agreement needs to be made clear. In Boorman's view the motivation should be "to fill a regulatory gap in the international institutional structure and, by making liberalization a purpose of the Fund and giving the Fund authority, to coordinate this activity better within the Fund and, perhaps, even provide the resources needed to carry out the associated responsibilities."

The IMF's Executive Board has discussed more formally reopening the issue of an amendment to the IMF Articles of Agreement with respect to capital account liberalization in the context of the Fund's medium-term strategy. Managing Director de Rato reported to the IMFC (IMF 2005f, 7): "[M]ost Directors did not wish to explore further at present the possibility (raised in 1996–97) of giving the Fund authority over capital movements, although a number of them felt that the Fund should be prepared to return to this issue at an appropriate time."

At the IMFC meeting on April 16, 2005, finance ministers from two G-7 countries, Gordon Brown (2005) from the United Kingdom and Domenico Siniscalco (2005) from Italy, expressed support for greater IMF activity in this area. On the other hand, Burhanuddin Abdullah (2005), governor of the Central Bank of Indonesia (speaking for a number of ASEAN countries), was firmly negative:

> On the issue of capital account liberalization, we are of the view that the Fund should not play a "central" role in this area. Past and recent experiences have clearly demonstrated that capital account restrictions are justified in some cases. At the same time, countries are already proceeding along the liberalization path, as they see fit, and as warranted by their own set of economic and financial circumstances. Therefore, the role for the Fund should be to ensure effective surveillance and that the necessary supporting infrastructure, especially adequate financial resources and appropriate financing instruments, are in place to help countries faced with capital account vulnerabilities or difficulties.

The Fund's role with respect to capital account liberalization, including the potential transitional role of restrictions on capital flows in particular for prudential reasons, is an important issue that the IMF will have to address more effectively. It is central to the IMF mission in the 21st century. It is also closely linked to the IMF's involvement in financial-sector issues.

Regional Arrangements

A final important area of the IMF's interface with the international monetary and financial system involves the Fund's relations and interaction with other formal or informal international organizations.

On the more formal side, first, are the Fund's relations with its sister Bretton Woods institution, the World Bank, where, despite frequent protestations to the contrary from the leadership of the two organizations, it is widely believed that turf battles are frequent and cooperation and coordination fall short of what a rational person would view as desirable.[13]

Second, relations with the Bank for International Settlements (BIS) at present are generally considered better than in the past largely because the BIS is seen less and less as a rival to the IMF.[14]

Third, relations with the WTO are uneven, and, as noted, one motivation for amending the IMF Articles of Agreement with respect to capital account liberalization was to establish the capital account as the IMF's turf at least with respect to financial flows and to prevent the WTO from extending its authority.

Fourth, the IMF has generally cordial relations with the Organization for Economic Cooperation and Development (OECD), with its more limited membership; here the competition is largely in the area of research and ideas.

Finally, the IMF's involvement with the regional development banks has been limited except in crisis situations during which the Fund itself or its major shareholders have sought to bring those institutions, in particular the Inter-American Development Bank and the Asian Development Bank, into consortia helping to provide financing to ameliorate external financial crises and to deal with the underlying policy challenges in member countries. On the other hand, the regional development banks have been known to support countries whose macroeconomic policies the IMF has faulted. The Asian Development Bank is also perceived to be a strong supporter of the establishment of an Asian Monetary Fund (AMF) as an alternative to the International Monetary Fund.

With respect to less formal organizations and nascent efforts to promote regional cooperation, the Fund's involvement is decidedly more ambiguous. For example, it is asserted (Zeti 2004) that it was Michel Camdessus who initially suggested in November 1996 in Jakarta that the East Asian

---

13. Turf battles and coordination are problems within the institutions as well.

14. A resolution passed at the Bretton Woods conference in 1944 called for the dissolution of the BIS, as did the US legislation approving the Bretton Woods agreements. Partly reflecting these sentiments, the Federal Reserve did not take up its seat on the BIS board until September 1994 (Siegman 1994). Since then the BIS has considerably expanded its membership and the scope of its activities, and it celebrated its 75th anniversary in 2005. However, the BIS no longer is involved in financing or helping to finance international rescue operations as it was from its inception through the late 1980s; it played a limited, window-dressing role in contributing to the Mexican package in 1995. Thus, the BIS and its central bank members collectively are not in direct competition with the IMF except in the area of ideas, for example, assessments of the global economy and critiques of crisis management. The BIS does provide a home for, and some of the resources to support the secretariat of, the Financial Stability Forum (FSF), which some within and outside the IMF see as a rival to the IMF as an institution of global financial governance.

economies get together and establish a process of regional surveillance along with a facility for mutual financial assistance.[15] When this proposal resurfaced less than a year later as a Japanese grandstand proposal for an AMF that would have been of no use in dealing with the East Asian financial crises because it would not come into existence for years, Camdessus was on the side of those who opposed the proposal. However, the proposal is not dead; it lives on in the form of the Chiang Mai Initiative and nascent Asian Bond Fund, and it has considerable support not only within the region but among certain people, including some within or close to the US government, who think that regional arrangements should shoulder a greater share of the general burden of emergency financing, in particular, and policy advice as well.

What should be the IMF's posture vis-à-vis such regional arrangements? Raghuram Rajan (2005a) has floated the idea that the IMF might seek the promotion of regional subsidiaries. If the regions with the mini-IMFs do not like being subsidiaries of a global institution in Washington dominated by the G-7 countries, how should the IMF seek to structure its relationship with independent organizations with essentially the same mandates to maintain economic and financial stability except in a regional context? Can one be confident that future external financial crises will have asymmetrical effects on countries in the region, facilitating mutual assistance, or will the crises continue to have symmetrical effects, rendering the possibility of such assistance nugatory? Can the global monetary system function effectively with more than one set of understandings, conventions, and rules, for example, about the trade-off between financing and adjustment or about the ultimate goal of capital account liberalization? In other words, is the global standard IMF conditionality or something weaker? These are big issues that the general membership of the IMF will not be able to continue to duck.

More prosaically, how should the IMF position itself vis-à-vis various efforts at regional integration? The European project has been ongoing for five decades. In East Asia, Africa, and Latin America integration efforts are more recent. The IMF now conducts formal regional surveillance exercises with respect to the euro area, the Central African Economic and Monetary Community, the West African Economic and Monetary Union, and the Eastern Caribbean Currency Union. In an era of scarce resources, the IMF might well want to scale back its surveillance activities with respect to the individual members of those regional arrangements while it concentrates on the larger units. At the same time, it might be expected to publish the documents that it produces in connection with its participation in peer-review processes such as the G-7 and various regional groups.

---

15. The official text ("Sustaining Macroeconomic Performance in the ASEAN Countries," an address to the Conference on Macroeconomic Issues Facing ASEAN Countries, Jakarta, Indonesia, November 7, 1996), published by the IMF, does not support this interpretation.

One particular topic that should be on the IMF's agenda with respect to its role in the international monetary system is the prospect that the euro may emerge as a serious rival to the US dollar as the principal international currency and international reserve currency. In recent years, the amount of verbal and, perhaps, financial speculation about international reserve diversification has increased dramatically. I have written about this issue (Truman 2005b). I have proposed an international reserve diversification standard that builds on the disclosure requirements with respect to international reserves (the "reserve template") in the IMF's Special Data Dissemination Standard (SDDS). Under this proposal, all major reserve holders would be expected regularly to disclose the currency composition of their foreign exchange reserves. In addition, they would be required to declare a benchmark, or adhere to a general benchmark, for the currency composition of their reserves. If they changed their benchmarks, they would commit to doing so only gradually over a period of, say, five years.[16] This would be a market-oriented approach to reserve diversification in contrast with earlier proposals to create an IMF substitution account to facilitate the relocation of reserves from dollars into SDRs last considered in 1979–80 (Boughton 2001, 936–43).

---

16. It would follow that marginal increases or decreases in foreign exchange reserves, as the result of intervention, should be allocated immediately according to the benchmark.

4

Governance

The IMF is an international institution established by an international agreement that is embedded in the legal systems of each member.[1] The institution is owned by and responsible to its member governments. Those governments, in turn, are responsible to their own citizens either in broad terms or more narrowly in the case of elected governments. Accountability, transparency, and legitimacy are at the core of the IMF existence vis-à-vis both its member governments and the world at large, regardless of how various governments or interest groups may agree or disagree on how those principles should be applied.

At the same time, the Fund is an institution of global cooperation and, I would argue, global governance, even though many observers reject that term. As such, the IMF is held responsible for its policies, actions, and inactions by international public opinion and the various groups that seek to influence or affect those opinions. This reality creates tension and controversy.

The emergence of a larger number of systemically significant countries during the past 60 years—especially the past 30 years—along with technological change that facilitates the instantaneous, global transmission of information—complete, incomplete, and distorted—has forced the IMF itself and its members to recognize the need for governance changes. Governance and balance in governance are important to the smooth functioning of the international financial system as a whole because if the IMF is respected, all countries have increased incentives to play by its common rules.

---

1. In the United States the governing law is the Bretton Woods Agreements Act first passed in 1945 and subsequently amended. Although in principle the international law incorporated in the IMF Articles of Agreement should take precedence over domestic law, in the few cases that have been decided in national courts, the IMF Articles have not always received that treatment.

IMF governance is a broad topic. A principal issue is the quotas of individual members. A second important issue involves the process of choosing the senior management of the institution. Third, IMF governance involves relationships among the governors of the IMF (who meet once a year but can be asked to vote by mail), the IMFC subset of governors (meeting twice a year), the Executive Board drawn from national capitals, the management, and the staff. A fourth important subtopic is the Executive Board itself, with respect to its powers, the qualifications of its members, the number of members, and the distribution of seats among the members of the IMF. The technical qualifications and geographic origins of the IMF staff might be regarded as management issues, but for some they are governance issues. Finally, under governance, one needs to consider how the institution as a whole relates to ad hoc groups, in particular groups of countries such as the G-7 industrial countries, the G-10 larger group of such countries, the G-11 group of developing countries, the G-20 combination of systemically important industrial and nonindustrial countries, as well as regional groups such as the European Union. In addition, self-appointed NGOs, academics, and other observers of the IMF's operations are quick to offer criticisms.

It is fair to argue, as did Williamson (2001, 109), that one should first decide what the Fund should do before addressing its governance. In principle, it should matter with respect to the governance of the Fund whether it is to be a smaller institution than it is today with limited lending and other responsibilities, a larger institution with an expanded mission and scope for lending, or remain the same. The view putting the horse before the cart is more pertinent to an institution that is just being established. The IMF has been around for more than 60 years, and the issue is how (whether) it should be reformed even though reforms are likely to be evolutionary.

Accepting that IMF reform may well be evolutionary, most observers agree that the IMF governance is a central element in any successful reform process that has any hope of restoring the Fund's global relevance.[2] The topic emerged with a vengeance during the East Asian financial crises when the affected countries felt that their problems were not addressed as generously and understandingly as they deserved, in part because the East Asian countries did not have the power and representation in the Fund that they merited on the basis of their economic importance.[3]

---

2. As noted above, Lawrence Summers in 1999 in a speech at the London School of Business commented on this topic in the context of a broader discussion of IMF reform as did the 1994 Bretton Woods Commission.

3. An alternative explanation for the level of support in the East Asian financial crises is that under the influence of European members that were critical of the scale of support that had been extended to Mexico, Fund management and staff were hesitant to propose large-scale lending. In fact, IMF commitments to Indonesia, Korea, and Thailand average 3.8 percent of

More recently, the Monterrey Consensus (UN 2002a) encouraged

> [t]he International Monetary Fund and World Bank to continue to enhance partic-
> ipation of all developing countries and countries with economies in transition in
> their decision-making, and thereby to strengthen the international dialogue and
> the work of those institutions as they address the development needs and con-
> cerns of these countries.

That encouragement has led to a number of discussions in the Development Committee (Joint Ministerial Committee of the Board of Governors of the Bank and the Fund on the Transfer of Real Resources to Developing Countries) on how to enhance the voice and participation of
developing and transition economies in the Fund and the Bank.

The leaders who gathered at Monterrey were not alone in the view that
governance should be on the agendas of the Bretton Woods institutions.
In one form or another, the topic was mentioned in September 2004 by 23
of the 60 who commented on how the structure of the Fund and the World
Bank should be changed (Emerging Markets 2004); this was, by far, the
most common of any of the responses.

The issues involved have been highlighted in reports of the managing
director to the IMFC and in the IMFC's communiqués.[4] The Group of 24
(G-24) ministers have been more strident (G-24 2005):

> Ministers note that the BWIs' [Bretton Woods institutions] governance structures
> have not evolved in line with the increased size and role of emerging market,
> developing, and transition countries in the world economy. Moreover, the role
> of small and low-income countries in the decision-making process is extremely
> limited. Ministers stress the need for concrete actions to reduce the democra-
> tic deficit and enhance the voice and participation of developing countries in
> decision-making at the IMF and World Bank, as called for in the Monterrey Con-
> sensus. They express disappointment that no progress has been made on this
> issue. The current under-representation of developing countries in the IMF and
> the World Bank Executive Boards undermines the legitimacy and effectiveness of
> these institutions.

The G-24 attaches sufficient attention to these issues that it has issued
an entire volume devoted to them (Buira 2005b).

Aside from the symbolism and power politics involved, IMF governance involves complex trade-offs between the legitimacy and opera-

---

GDP compared with 4.6 percent for Mexico, but IMF plus bilateral commitments averaged
9.0 percent of GDP compared with 9.6 percent for Mexico (Roubini and Setser 2004, 125).
This is not necessarily the right metric because it makes no adjustment for need or circumstances, but it suggests that the Asian complaint and the European conspiracy view are not
broadly supported by the data.

4. "The IMF's effectiveness and credibility as a cooperative institution must be safeguarded
and further enhanced. Adequate voice and participation by all members should be assured,
and the distribution of quotas should reflect developments in the world economy" (IMFC
2005).

tional efficiency of the Fund in conducting its business (Cottarelli 2005). Choices have to be made if there is to be progress on overall IMF reform. The IMF will not be able to continue successfully without adjustments in its governance structures. Lane (2005) links action on various governance issues to the resolution of tensions within the Fund concerning such contentious issues as how best to deal with emerging-market crises, the proper scope of IMF conditionality, the phenomenon of prolonged use of IMF resources, and the IMF's relationship with low-income countries.

The balance of this chapter looks at four aspects of IMF governance: (1) shares of IMF quotas, (2) choosing IMF management and staff, (3) reforming the Executive Board, in particular, the distribution of seats (chairs) on the board, and (4) the IMF's relations with various international steering groups.

Quotas and Voting Power

IMF quotas are the principal issue in IMF governance because quotas are the building blocks for many aspects of the IMF and its operations. A country's quota directly translates into voting power because the number of votes a country has in the Fund is based primarily on the size of its quota.[5] What matters is not the total number of votes, of course, but the relative size of quotas because formal voting is generally by weighted majority with most issues requiring only a simple weighted majority; a few issues require either 70 percent or 85 percent majorities.[6] The United States, with the largest quota, has 17.08 percent of the votes, and therefore can block (veto) change on the last set of issues.[7] In addition, a member's quota fixes how much that country may be called upon to lend to other members through the Fund. It also determines more loosely how much a member can borrow from the Fund.

The size of the Fund in terms of total quotas in the Fund must be reviewed at least every five years. Some of those reviews have been prolonged beyond five years.[8] Roughly half—8 of 13—of the reviews have resulted in an increase in the size of the Fund.[9] Currently the IMF is in its

---

5. A member has 250 basic votes regardless of the size of its quota and one vote per 100,000 SDR of its quota.

6. Amendment of the IMF Articles of Agreement requires a weighted majority of 85 percent of members and the positive votes of 60 percent of members.

7. The US quota in the IMF is 371,493 hundred thousand SDR. As of August 2005, its quota share was 17.40 percent.

8. One review was concluded inside the five-year window.

9. New members of the Fund are given quotas commensurate with the size of quotas of existing members (often a complex negotiation), which increases the overall size of the Fund while reducing the quotas and voting shares of existing members.

13th quota review cycle, which is scheduled to be completed by January 2008. Aside from determining the overall size of the Fund, a review that involves an increase in overall quotas can affect the relative size of quotas and therefore a country's voting power.

Negotiations over IMF quotas have traditionally been informed by formulas that involve

- GDP at current market prices (an indicator of economic size and of a country's capacity to contribute to the Fund),

- official international reserves (an indicator of a country's capacity to contribute to the Fund),

- current payments (an indicator of openness as well as of potential need to borrow from the Fund),

- current receipts (another indicator of openness as well as of potential need to borrow from the Fund), and

- the variability of current receipts (another indicator of potential need to borrow from the Fund).

These five variables are measured, often with difficulty, over periods of varying length and combined according to a variety of different weights.[10] Starting with the Eighth Review of Quotas in 1983, five different formulas have been used to generate calculated quotas. Calculated quotas often differ substantially from actual quotas because of the tension between actual historical quotas and differences in the pace of countries' economic development.[11] An adjustment factor is applied to the results of each formula so that they yield the same overall total. A country's calculated quota is the larger of the original "Bretton Woods formula" and the average of the two smallest of the four remaining formulas, appropriately scaled. In most quota reviews that result in an increase in total quotas, the increase in a country's individual quota is composed of some combination of its current quota share, an adjustment to bring some or all countries closer to their calculated quota shares, and occasionally ad hoc adjustments for countries whose quotas are way out of line. Everything is scaled to the new overall size of the Fund.

In the 2004 estimates, a distribution of quota shares based on calculated quotas would boost the share of advanced countries 6.7 percentage points relative to actual quota shares and reduce the shares of developing

---

10. In many cases, data have to be estimated. In addition, in recent discussions and calculations the last variable is calculated as the variability of current receipts and net capital inflows.

11. The historical relationship dates back to the Bretton Woods conference in 1944, when a formula was used as a guideline for establishing initial IMF quotas, but the results of the formula were only indicative. A political agreement was required to set the quotas for the important countries and establish their relative quota shares along with the formula itself.

countries 3.9 percentage points and transition economies 2.8 percentage points (IMF 2004g).[12] However, within the group of developing countries, the calculated quota share for the subgroup of Asia (including Korea and Singapore) would be 4.6 percent points higher than its actual share of 10.3 percent.

Moreover, within each category of countries, a distribution of IMF quotas based on calculated quotas would bring about large adjustments in relative voting power. In the 2004 estimates, the US share would rise 2.4 percent, Germany's would rise 15.3 percent, but France's would decline 13.1 percent. Among developing countries, China's share would rise 55.5 percent, India's would decline 47.3 percent, and Venezuela's would decline 67.4 percent; but Mexico's would rise 57.4 percent and Korea's 177.4 percent, which would make it the 11th largest quota in the Fund. Among transition economies, Russia's share would decline 52.3 percent, but the Czech Republic's share would be boosted 18.4 percent. The sizes of these differences reflect a combination of inertia that anchors shares in historical relationships with each other and differential rates of economic and financial development.

Vijay Kelkar et al. (2005) dramatically point to some of the voting power anomalies associated, in their view, with the current quota structure.[13] They note that the combined votes on the IMF Executive Board of Brazil, China, and India are 19 percent less than the combined votes of Belgium, Italy, and the Netherlands at the same time (2000–01) that their combined GDPs at market exchange rates are 23 percent higher, their GDPs at purchasing power parity (2000 PPP estimates) are four times higher, and their populations are 29 times higher. Note, however, that the percentage difference between the combined calculated quota shares of the two groups of countries, based on data through 2002 (IMF 2004g), would be unchanged from the percentage difference in their combined actual quotas.[14]

The quota formulas themselves are subject to the same conflicting forces of inertia and of differences in the pace of countries' economic and financial development.[15] Consequently, many members of the IMF advocate changing the quota formulas to simplify the formula, preferably to

---

12. In these calculations, the current quota share of advanced countries (for these purposes, industrial countries plus Cyprus and Israel) is 61.6 percent, the share of developing countries is 30.9 percent, and the share of transition economies is 7.5 percent.

13. Vijay Kelkar has coauthored a number of papers on IMF governance; see references, including Kelkar, Yadev, and Chaudhry (2004).

14. The calculated quota shares of Italy and the Netherlands are larger than their current actual quotas, outweighing the implied decline in Belgium's quota; at the same time, the large increase in China's calculated quota is partially offset by large decreases in the calculated quotas of India and Brazil.

15. Dirk Messner et al. (2005) propose increasing the weight of developing countries' votes in the IMF and at the same time revising the IMF Articles of Agreement so that the voting

one standard with no more than four variables, and to update the variables. Not surprisingly, this is not an exact science.

In 2000, an outside committee chaired by Richard Cooper (IMF 2000) recommended a simplified formula based on two variables: GDP (the potential ability to contribute to the Fund) and the variability of current receipts and net long-term capital flows (an alternative measure of the potential need to borrow from the Fund), with the coefficient on the former twice that on the latter composite. This proposal did not attract a lot of support inside or outside of the IMF.

Others (such as Kelkar with his various coauthors) have suggested replacing GDP at market prices and current exchange rates with GDP on a PPP basis, which ceteris paribus would tend to boost the quota shares of developing countries. Bryant (2004) proposes including population in the formula along with GDP. Introducing this variable would also increase the voting power in the IMF of developing countries as a group but would benefit poorer developing countries relative to the voting power of richer developing countries.

Even technical adjustments in the way the quota formulas have been estimated can matter; Buira (2005a, 27) reports that excluding intra-area trade in the calculated quotas of the 12 euro area members of the IMF would reduce their combined calculated quota share by 11.4 percentage points.[16] On the other hand, the latest estimated calculated quotas reported by the IMF (2004g) would boost the combined quota share of the euro area by 4.5 percentage points relative to those countries' combined share of actual quotas. Thus, if EU and euro area quotas are to be reduced, as many have called for, either the quota formula will have to be changed or the interpretation of the inputs will have to be substantially modified, for example, with respect to intra-EU trade.

A large group of small countries is particularly interested in adjusting the number of basic votes for each member of the IMF, now 250 votes per country. It is pointed out (Buira 2005a; Kelkar et al. 2005; Kelkar, Chaudhry, and Vanduzer-Snow 2005) that basic votes represented about 11 percent of total votes in 1945 and represent 2 percent today. The number of basic votes per member has been unchanged and the number of members of the IMF has increased substantially, but the increase in the overall size of quotas has swamped the latter effect. (An amendment of the IMF Articles of

---

shares would be recalibrated every 10 years. The problem, of course, is that the formula used to increase the weight of developing countries could also lead to a reduction of their weight at the time of recalibration.

16. Lorenzo Bini Smaghi (2004) has a similar result, a reduction in calculated quotas of 11.7 percentage points and a reduction in voting power of 9.1 percentage points for the euro area. For the 25 current members of the European Union (EU-25), Bini Smaghi estimates that the reduction in calculated quotas would be 15.1 percentage points, and the reduction in voting power 12.6 percentage points, from which the US voting power would receive a boost of 4.2 percentage points.

Agreement would be required to change the number of basic votes each country would receive.) Kelkar at al. (2005) calculate that if there were an increase in basic votes that restored their share of total votes to 11.3 percent, and if the remaining 89.7 percent of quota shares were distributed according to GDP on a PPP basis, the voting share of developing countries would rise by 11.5 percentage points, with the group shares of developing countries in Africa, Asia, and the Western Hemisphere all rising, and the voting share of advanced countries declining 10.8 percentage points. Moreover, the US voting share would increase 2 percentage points, more than preserving the US veto.[17]

On the other hand, adjusting the number of basic votes each country receives would not do much for most groups of countries. Ngaire Woods and Domenico Lombardi (2005) point out that the voting share of the largest 24-country African constituency would rise from 1.99 percent to only 2.81 percent. Merely adjusting basic votes is a feel-good solution to the problem of voting power in the IMF as well as a high-cost solution because it would require an amendment of the IMF Articles of Agreement. Woods and Lombardi propose a more radical reform involving expanding the double-majority approach, in which certain decisions require various weighted majority votes plus various majorities of members. This could increase the scope to block specific changes, but it could well make it more difficult to implement change except as part of a carefully assembled package of proposals. However, it would potentially increase the leverage of the sub-Saharan African countries whose two constituencies include 43 countries, 24 percent of the total membership of the Fund.

Because the United States has more than 15 percent of the votes, it can block (veto) certain major decisions of the IMF; however, very few affect the ongoing operations of the IMF. Nevertheless, many observers feel that the US veto gives the United States undue leverage over the day-to-day decisions in the IMF.[18] However, the United States could only voluntarily lose its veto because it could always block any amendment of the IMF Articles of Agreement or quota increase that had the effect of reducing the US voting share below 15 percent.[19] In the context of the second amend-

---

17. The US voting share would decline about 1.5 percentage points but remain above 15 percent if the contribution of basic votes to total votes were restored to the 1945 level. This decline would be more than offset by the switch to quota shares based only on PPP-based GDP.

18. The basis for the presumption is understandable, but I have witnessed too many cases where the IMF has not followed US wishes to worry a great deal about such problems. What is true is that the United States historically has cared consistently about the IMF as an institution and about its day-to-day operations.

19. In principle, it might be possible to admit by majority vote enough new members with large enough quotas to drive the US voting share below 15 percent, but that would take an increase in IMF quotas of more than 14 percent via such a process. There are not enough nonmember countries in the world to generate such an increase where each new member's quota is constrained by the size of the quotas of comparable countries, based on the five quota formulas scaled to the current size of the IMF.

ment to the IMF Articles of Agreement in 1978, the majority for deciding some issues was raised from 80 to 85 percent. This facilitated a reduction in the US voting share from above 20 percent to above 15 percent while preserving the US veto. Most proposed adjustments in the quota formula, aside from those introducing a heavy weight on population or international reserves, would not adversely affect the US quota share. While a case can be made that it is in the US interest to reduce its quota share voluntarily so that it no longer can be accused of having undue influence over the Fund, such an action is far from likely except in the context of a very large package of IMF reforms that the United States strongly supports.

A potentially more promising route would involve the establishment of a single EU or euro area constituency that would also have more than 15 percent voting power, creating a "contestable" veto power with identical quotas for the United States and the European Union. If their voting shares were both about 18 percent of the overall total, it would free up about 13 percentage points to reallocate to other countries reflecting their relative economic development.[20] Alternatively, both the United States and the European Union could agree to reduce their voting power below 15 percent as part of a grand bargain on IMF reform whose outlines at this point are decidedly blurred. This would free up an even larger share of quotas and votes for reallocation.

Notwithstanding the political and technical complexities, the issue of the relative size of quotas and voting power is central to reforming IMF governance. Jack Boorman, in his remarks to an Institute of International Finance Seminar in London on November 17, 2004, argued that the Europeans must take the lead. I have argued (Boyer and Truman 2005; Truman 2005a) that the United States has some leverage, albeit in the nuclear category, on the European position. Every two years, the United States has an opportunity to block the continuation of the Executive Board at its current size of 24 seats, rather than the 20 called for in the IMF Articles, because the vote to continue to raise the number of seats to 24 requires an 85 percent (weighted) majority.

Europe holds the key to progress in this area, and the pressure is rising. Burhanuddin Abdullah (2005) expressed in unusually strong terms the frustration on this issue felt by East Asian countries:

> Finally and most importantly, we stress the criticality of addressing serious shortcomings in the Fund's governance structure, as well as a lack of sense of ownership of some members. In order to enhance the effectiveness and legitimacy of the Fund, all members of the institution must feel a sense of ownership. They must feel well represented and that they have a say in decisions taken by the Fund. As such, all members should have adequate voice and participation.
>
> In this regard, our constituency strongly believes that countries' quota shares have to be reviewed and updated so that they reflect countries' relative positions in the world economy. A viable solution could be a rebalancing of quotas within

---

20. EU countries currently have 32 percent of IMF votes.

the existing total, whereby countries that are overweighted could voluntarily transfer quota shares to countries that have grown quickly due to successful economic performance and are now grossly underrepresented. Without advancement in such an important area, the Fund's credibility will continue to be undermined due to the monopolistic behavior of large countries with veto power. In particular, the Fund runs the serious risk of losing its relevance in Asia unless the Fund effectively engages Asian countries by addressing this issue of the lack of voice and effective participation in the decision-making process. The influence, credibility, and legitimacy of the Fund are contingent upon these changes. In this light, the upcoming 13th General Review of Quotas will provide an opportune time to achieve this objective, which should not be delayed any further. The ultimate goal is to see a Fund that performs important functions for the benefit of all member countries and cherishes the practice of consensus building in reaching board decisions.

The ASEAN+3 (China, Japan, and Korea are the +3) finance ministers in May 2005 pledged to work together on this issue. The trilateral finance ministers (China, Japan, and Korea alone) made a similar statement at the same time. The Japanese Finance Minister Sadakazu Tanigaki (2005) had already spoken eloquently about this topic in April: "The IMF needs to listen and understand the frustration and concerns Asian countries feel toward it and make serious efforts to address these concerns. Unless the IMF responds effectively to the above, it could irrevocably lose relevance in Asia and ultimately in the world." He cited two concerns: first, Asian countries' status in the IMF in terms of the distribution of quotas, board members, and staff, and second, whether the institution is making sufficient efforts to prevent, manage, and resolve capital account crises.[21]

The United States has taken a forward-leaning position on this issue. At the IMFC meeting in April 2005, US Treasury Secretary John Snow (2005) stated:

> We believe the time is ripe to start considering how to address these inter-related issues [IMF representation should evolve along with the evolution of the world economy and the world economy is now ahead of the evolution of the IMF]. The IMF's liquidity is at an all-time high. But the fact that the IMF does not need an increase in its resources need not impede change. A rebalancing of quotas from "over-represented" countries to the "under-represented" within the existing total could yield substantial progress. This will not be an easy task, but it can be achieved with boldness and vision to help modernize the Fund.

These are clearly complex issues, and careful consideration and consultation are needed to address the full range of concerns. This is important to preserving the global character of the IMF, so that all countries feel they have a rightful stake in the institution.

US Acting Under Secretary Randal Quarles (2005) reiterated the US position in June 2005, including a statement that "progress should not, and

---

21. Tanigaki did not put forward in his written statement the proposal, which had been attributed in the press to the Japanese government in advance of the meeting of the IMFC, that ASEAN+3 quotas in the IMF should be increased from 13 percent to 20 percent.

indeed need not, be linked to an increase in the IMF's quota resources." Given the rancorous history of IMF quota negotiations, the US position is naive at best and cynical at worst. This is the case even if the US position is driven by strategic considerations and US government officials recognize that in the end an adjustment in quota shares will only occur in the context of an increase in the overall size of the Fund. The reason the US position looks as if it is just for show is that individual member countries must consent to any reduction in their quotas. It is highly unlikely that any country will voluntarily reduce its quota so that the amount can be transferred to another country. Moreover, the European countries collectively have more than enough votes to block any increase in total IMF quotas that would result in a reallocation of quota shares that does not satisfy them.

The common EU position on this issue at this point is not forward leaning. Jean-Claude Junker (2005) stated the EU position at the April IMFC:

> EU countries support this process [of strengthening the participation of developing countries] and welcome the steps that have been taken so far by the IMF and the World Bank to strengthen the voice of developing and transition countries as well as the renewed focus from IMF management on the importance of this issue. At the same time it is important to discuss further measures, such as initiatives to further build policy capacity in developing countries, further enhancement of delegation office capacity and overall general measures such as an increase in basic votes.

Note that Junker did not mention reducing the quotas or quota shares of EU members of the IMF. Such an offer will have to wait at least until the hard bargaining begins.

Choice of Management and Staff

The processes used today to choose the managing director of the Fund and the president of the World Bank satisfy few observers, with the important exception of key senior officials and political leaders in the United States and in Europe. The Executive Boards of the two organizations in principle elect the heads of the organizations. In practice, with a few variations around the edges, the existing convention, by agreement between the United States and (a growing) Europe is that the Europeans propose the managing director of the IMF by an ad hoc internal process and the US president proposes the president of the World Bank. The Executive Boards subsequently deliberate and elect the individuals proposed. This convention dates back to the founding of the institutions. It has been widely criticized for decades, but it persists. Since 1999 two new managing directors of the IMF and one new president of the World Bank have been chosen on the basis of the convention.

Miles Kahler (2001) put forward the most comprehensive proposal for change in this area. His proposal calls for (1) abandoning the US-European convention, (2) establishing a selection process based on developed criteria, (3) expanding the list of candidates to include internal candidates, (4) placing the selection process squarely, rather than indirectly, in the hands of ministers, (5) developing a long list of candidates and later a veto-proof short list of candidates, and (6) reinforcing the process via a two-term limit and a review process at the end of the first term.

Many others advocate change. In the wake of widespread dissatisfaction with the process that resulted in the choice of Horst Köhler as the IMF managing director in 2000, the executive directors of the Bank and the Fund formed working groups to reform the selection processes for the heads of the two organizations (Kahler 2001, 77–78). Those groups did not recommend discarding the US-European convention (IMFC 2001). Instead, they recommended other changes to the selection process that would involve a more transparent process of choosing the heads of the organizations. The two Executive Boards endorsed the report in April 2001 as guidance for the process, and IMFC noted the report in its communiqué. However, these efforts had no visible influence on the processes that subsequently led to Rodrigo de Rato's succeeding Horst Köhler in 2004 and Paul Wolfowitz's succeeding James Wolfensohn in 2005.

In an interview as he left the World Bank, Wolfensohn (*The New York Times*, May 25, 2005, C5) endorsed a selection process for the Bank in which the president would be selected from a range of candidates in a transparent way: "I would personally wish that one could make these appointments on merit." Horst Köhler (IMF 2004h), when he left the IMF, expressed his support for a more transparent selection process that is not limited to a particular country or region although he acknowledged that there would always be an element of politics in the process. David Peretz (2005, 27) advocates modifying the process for selecting the managing director of the IMF by taking it out of the hands of member governments and charging a group of "wise men [and women]" to come up with a range of possibilities and appointing the best person for the job regardless of nationality. He also notes that reform of the selection process for the head of the IMF depends on reforms in the selection process for choosing the head of the World Bank and the World Trade Organization, which did modify its procedure somewhat in 2005. The issues involved apply as well to choosing the heads of UN agencies (where the UNDP used an open model in 2005), the OECD, the BIS, and the regional development banks.[22]

Questions about the selection of the managing director of the IMF extend to the selection of the deputy managing directors and the diversity of the staff. The first deputy managing director of the IMF, according to the

---

22. The president of the Inter-American Development Bank traditionally comes from Latin America, and the president of the African Development Bank comes from Africa. However, the president of the European Bank for Reconstruction and Development comes from Western Europe (with the number two position reserved for a US national), and the Japanese nominate the president of the Asian Development Bank.

US-European convention, comes from the United States. Until the mid-1990s, the managing director had only one deputy managing director (DMD). When Stanley Fischer was selected, the number of DMDs was expanded to include two others. To date, two of the DMDs have come from Japan, two have come from Latin America, one has come from India, and one from Africa.

Many members of the IMF complain about a lack of diversity within the senior staff and the staff as a whole. They argue that those positions tend to be occupied by people from what are now viewed as creditor countries, thus providing such countries with undue influence over IMF policies and decisions on programs of financial support. With respect to skills, most observers believe that IMF staff hiring and promotion are merit based; most of the technical skills involved are universal, not national or regional. The issue of influence by the governments of the staff's country of origin is more complex.

The concerns are three. The first concern is about the power and influence of IMF technocrats who are viewed as economists trained in a particular analytical tradition. Most people familiar with disputes among economists and the lack of a Washington Consensus find this concern overblown although they do not dispute the technocratic foundation of much of the IMF's work and the influence of technocrats in the organization.

The second concern is geographic diversity. A concern for diversity need not distort a merit-based appointment and promotion process. However, it can well have that effect. Today, the IMF imposes informal limits on hiring nationals from some countries. Despite its very competitive salaries favoring nationals of countries other than the United States, it often has difficulty attracting qualified applicants to Washington.

The third concern is about political influence. Only a fool would argue that politics never enters into decisions by IMF staff and, in particular, by management, but many observers (Bird 2003; Bird and Rowlands 2001; Cottarelli 2005; Van Houtven 2002) conclude that there is limited evidence of systematic political influence in IMF decisions. Some scholars (Barro and Lee 2002) have found some evidence of political influence. However, their findings are sensitive to specification of the time period and the definition of evidence of influence. As described in Woods and Lombardi (2005), the IMF faces a large number of different types of decisions with the result that at times there may be a strong consensus on those issues; at other times, shifting coalitions of countries push particular programs or views.

Chairs and Reform of the Executive Board

The Executive Board of the International Monetary Fund is charged with the supervision of the activities of the institution. The executive directors are appointed or elected by member governments. They are paid by the

Fund. As such, their roles are somewhat ambiguous. Are they to represent the views of the governments that chose them or the interests of the institution as a whole when those interests diverge? Does the role of the board need to be strengthened (Van Houtven 2004)? Should its scope and powers be broadened (Rajan 2005a)? Should its size be increased to reflect the increased membership of the Fund or should its size be reduced or seats reallocated to make it more efficient or representative?

Peter Kenen et al. (2004), David Peretz (2005), and Raghuram Rajan (2005a) either favor or are favorably inclined toward a nonresident Executive Board, with senior officials from capitals meeting regularly—but certainly not the current three days a week—to make important decisions. This reform would tend to strengthen the role of the staff and management of the Fund at the same time that it would receive more overt political direction on key issues.

José De Gregorio et al. (1999) advocate a board independent of governments in the model of independent central banks. Timothy Lane (2005) sensibly criticizes this view. He argues that independent central banks have reasonably well-defined objectives focused more or less precisely on price stability. Evaluation of the performance of the IMF involves determining whether the institution's advice was sound and whether it was appropriate for the Fund to lend to particular countries in particular circumstances. Those are questions that require judgment ex ante and later invite second-guessing without agreed quantitative tests that can be applied.

Vijay L. Kelkar et al. (2005) and Kelkar, Chaudhry, and Vanduzer-Snow (2005) advocate an intermediate solution in which each executive director would serve a fixed six-year term and would be responsible to his or her parliament or parliaments.[23] Some observers favor other steps to increase the transparency and accountability of the Executive Board. For example, Woods and Lombardi (2005) favor the prompt publication of executive directors' votes and the positions they take as well as evaluations of their performance against standards set by the countries that elected them.

The IMF Executive Board at present has 24 members. Some, for example Jack Boorman in remarks in London on November 17, 2004, think the board is too large; Peretz (2005) calls for a reduction to 15 seats. Woods and Lombardi (2005) favor a more even distribution of countries and seats. They advocate that each of the three executive directors elected by single countries (China, Russia, and Saudi Arabia) should take more countries

---

23. Kelkar et al. (2005) and Woods and Lombardi (2005) single out the United States for setting a good example with respect to the accountability of its executive director because the US executive director is nominated by the president and confirmed by the US Senate, and the person can be called to testify before the Congress. (Some other executive directors testify before parliaments; see, for example, Lynch [2005].) The US executive director also is obligated to serve at a reduced salary partly as a consequence of the person's exposed political position. Moreover, the US executive director serves at the pleasure of the president and conventionally is replaced soon after a change in US administration.

into their constituencies. They estimate that the resulting reallocation of countries and constituencies could reduce the size of each one to no more than 10 countries. As a subsequent step, if other countries choose to be represented by one of the five appointed executive directors, the number of countries in each constituency could be reduced further, to no more than eight.[24] The result, they speculate, might be that the elected executive directors would become more independent of their national governments.

If IMF constituencies became more equal in size and voting power, it would still not solve the issue of the redistribution of voting power. Boyer and Truman (2005) and Truman (2005a) have advocated addressing the issue of chairs (IMF representation) and shares (the distribution of votes) as part of a process focused primarily on the members of the IMF that are also members of the European Union. At present the 25 EU countries appoint or play a major role in the election of 10 of the 24 IMF executive directors, 42 percent of the Executive Board. Among the 10, they currently supply 6 executive directors and 8 alternate executive directors—29 percent of the total. In five cases they supply both. In brief, the European Union is overrepresented on an Executive Board that traditionally reaches decisions via consensus; the European voices are too many and as a consequence receive too much weight. EU members also directly control 32 percent of the votes in the IMF.[25] Indirectly through the inclusion of non-EU countries in their constituencies or the presence of EU countries in non-EU-majority constituencies, the European Union potentially can influence an additional 12.5 percent for a total of almost 45 percent.

Rationalizing the allocation of shares and chairs within the IMF in principle involves two separable issues, one having to do with shares and the other having to do with chairs. In practice, both issues will almost certainly have to be addressed at the same time even if progress toward the ultimate goals of these reforms involves different timetables. Shares will have to be reallocated toward those countries whose relative economic size has outstripped the relative size of their quotas, generally the large emerging-market economies (LEMs). Such a shift would tend to support the financial stability of the organization.

The reallocation of chairs is a more complicated process. Boyer and Truman (2005) and Truman (2005a) advocate a multistep process. First, countries that are not members of the European Union and do not aspire to EU membership would join other constituencies, and EU members such as Ireland, Poland, and Spain would join EU constituencies. This would probably reduce the number of EU or potential EU executive directors and alternate executive directors from a potential of 10 each to 6 or 7 each. Non-EU executive directors and alternate executive directors in reconstituted con-

---

24. The authors are vague about whether such a change would require an amendment of the IMF Articles of Agreement, but that almost certainly would be the case.

25. The 10 new EU members that joined in May 2004 have only 2.1 percent of the votes.

stituencies would occupy the freed-up seats. As a second step or series of steps, the EU chairs would be consolidated into one chair; this would allow for the establishment of new constituencies or for a smaller Executive Board. The complexity of working out this realignment to the reasonable satisfaction of most IMF members should not be underestimated. No country should end up not being represented, and large countries should resist limiting the size of their constituencies to the minimum number of votes necessary to claim a seat.

Miles Kahler (2001) also advocates a consolidation of EU chairs in the IMF. Peter B. Kenen et al. (2004) do so as well. However, Kenen at al. would stop the process, as the situation now stands, at two chairs, one for the euro area and one for non–euro area EU-member countries.

Many observers from a European perspective (Bini Smaghi 2004; Woods and Lombardi 2005; and Willy Kiekens in remarks, "What Kind of External Representation for the Euro?" delivered at an Austrian National Bank seminar on June 2, 2003) see the consolidation of EU representation into a single chair as a positive step in Europe's interests. Horst Köhler (IMF 2004h) expressed support for an ever-closer political union within Europe and saw consolidating EU chairs in the IMF as consistent with that vision. Since the Vienna European Council meeting in December 1998, EU members have sought to upgrade the coordination of their positions in international forums, the IMF in particular. From the bottom up, IMF executive directors from EU countries meet in Washington with representatives of the European Central Bank (ECB) and the European Commission as the EURIMF. Further up the line, a staff group (subcommittee on IMF matters, or SCIMF) involving national capitals as well as the ECB and the Commission works up common positions for subsequent review and approval by the Economic and Financial Committee (EFC) of deputies and final review and approval by the Council of EU Finance Ministers (Ecofin) (Bini Smaghi 2004; Woods and Lombardi 2005). However, partly because of the presence of non-EU members in some constituencies and the presence of other constituencies in which EU members are not dominant and partly because of the desire of some EU members to go their own ways on some IMF issues, this process of coordination has not produced uniform EU positions on all issues.

As noted earlier in connection with the issue of the distribution of IMF quotas in the IMF, the Europeans properly should take the lead in this area. To date, they are not so inclined, if one can judge by what Junker (2005) said to the IMFC. To break this logjam, the United States has its nuclear option.[26] However, an important question is whether the United

---

26. In principle, any group of countries with more than 15 percent of IMF voting power has similar leverage to force a reallocation of chairs within the IMF. However, the direct consequences of failure would be larger because, if the size of the Executive Board were reduced to 20 seats without a consolidation of European seats, the instigators might find themselves without any representation on the board.

States sees it in its interest to deal with a single European entity. In Truman (2005a) I argue in the affirmative and that the United States in general should push for closer European integration. However, not all US officials and observers agree. Each camp can interpret the constitutional issues that arose in the late spring of 2005 as favoring its initial position.

If the Europeans were to consolidate their representation in the IMF, such a step would have strong implications for the IMF as an institution, including other aspects of its governance (Mathieu, Ooms, and Rottier 2003). Note one aspect: according to the current Articles of Agreement, if the European Union were to assume a consolidated chair as a single country, which some argue would require an amendment of the IMF Articles of Agreement, and the EU quota were the largest in the IMF, the headquarters of the IMF would have to be moved to Europe. Such a move might cause considerable disruption, but that possibility would be one that would have to be addressed as part of an overall bargain.

The IMF and Steering Committees

A basic question with respect to IMF governance is from where does the institution receive its direction? Today, as a formal matter, the IMF management runs the Fund. The Executive Board supervises the management and staff. The IMFC is formally an advisory body that in effect provides some overall guidance.[27] The Board of Governors acts in the areas where the Articles of Agreement require it to act.

In practice, none of these groups acts as a true steering committee for the IMF. One might well argue that the IMFC should play this role. However, despite efforts in recent years to bolster its role, it has failed as a body that either generates consensus or provides broad innovative direction to the Fund. That role has been played by outside steering committees. Only a trained political scientist can explain this failure, and colleagues of that political scientist would probably disagree. This observer's explanation is that the IMFC's effectiveness is constrained by two factors: (1) the continuing formality of its meetings, complete with speeches that are prepared in advance and released to the public, and (2) the substantial control over the IMFC's agenda and discussion that is exercised by IMF management and staff.

---

27. The French finance minister, Thierry Breton (2005), proposed the revival of the proposal to institute the Council, as provided in the IMF Articles of Agreement, as a body representing the Board of Governors with formal decision-making power in the IMF, replacing the advisory IMFC. Such a step would tend further to weaken the IMF Executive Board and strengthen the role of the IMF management and staff. However, that proposal was reconsidered and set aside in the late 1990s, when the Interim Committee, intended as a precursor of the Council, was transformed into the IMFC.

Throughout its history, the IMF management and staff itself have not been a principal source of innovation or direction for the international economic and financial system. The G-10 negotiated the Smithsonian Agreement, and the IMF's involvement in that negotiation lost the managing director his job. The ad hoc Committee of Twenty (C-20) dealt as best it could with the IMF reform process following the Smithsonian Agreement. The IMF has not been able, or allowed, to play a major role in shaping cooperation on major international macroeconomic policy issues.[28] The reasons for this weakness are complex. The IMF has been ineffective, in part, because its most powerful members wanted it that way. The IMF also is an institution that is dominated by its staff, which means that it is cautious with respect to innovation. At the same time, the IMF has not been able, despite repeated efforts, to sponsor effective dialogue outside of a narrow interpretation of the scope of its responsibilities.

Over the past 30-plus years, the steering committee of the IMF was first the G-10 with a strong US lead, next the G-5 countries, and more recently the G-7 countries.[29] Of course, the G-7 finance ministers and central bank governors seek to steer the international financial system and the global economy, not just the International Monetary Fund, but in the process they have been the steering committee for the IMF as well.

C. Fred Bergsten, in a March 4, 2004, speech in Leipzig, Germany, to the deputies of the G-20 on the subject of the G-20 and the world economy, Boyer and Truman (2005), and Truman (2005a) have called upon the G-20 to replace the G-7 in its role as the steering committee for the international financial system and the IMF.[30] As noted earlier, Lawrence Summers in December 1999 delivered a speech at the London School of Business in which he called for the G-20 to play an operational role in the international financial system, but to date its operational role has been strictly circumscribed by tacit agreement within the G-7.

Mervyn King, in remarks at a conference on February 4, 2005, stressed the need to expand the group of countries that discusses exchange rate and other macroeconomic policy issues beyond the G-7. He might stop at a G-7 group plus a few other countries, such as China and India or the five

---

28. The IMF has played a major and sometimes innovative, if controversial, role in connection with some specific issues, for example, the debt crises of the 1980s and the transformation of the economies of Eastern Europe and the former Soviet Union in the 1990s.

29. The G-5 includes France, Germany, Japan, the United Kingdom, and the United States. The finance G-7 includes also Canada and Italy. (The G-8 includes Russia, but it is principally a political group.) The G-10 includes Belgium, the Netherlands, Sweden, and Switzerland as well as the G-7.

30. The industrial-country members of the G-20 comprise the G-7, Australia, and the country holding the EU presidency when that is not a European G-7 country; nonindustrial-country members are Argentina, Brazil, China, India, Indonesia, Korea, Mexico, Russia, Saudi Arabia, South Africa, and Turkey.

countries (Brazil, China, India, Mexico, and South Africa) that joined the G-8 at their leaders' summit in Gleneagles, Scotland, in July 2005. During 2005, Brazil, China, India, and South Africa participated in several meetings of the finance G-7. However, although they were invited as more than breakfast or luncheon guests, the finance ministers and central bank governors of those countries were not full participants in the meetings in the sense that they were not involved in the full agenda of issues, including drafting the final communiqué in which the G-7's conclusions, agreements, and directives are enunciated.

The G-20 is a more natural group to play a significant role as a global steering committee in light of the changing and broadening list of countries of systemic importance, a list that extends beyond Brazil, China, India, and South Africa for many issues such as energy, global adjustment, and governance more generally.[31] Central bankers actively participate in G-20 meetings alongside finance ministers; this feature contributes to the group's permanence as well as to its technical expertise on international economic and financial issues. With a group as large as 20, subcaucuses on specific issues would be expected. If the G-20 is to have more influence, a permanent secretariat might be desirable along with the use of working groups and more frequent deputies' meetings to follow up on ministerial decisions.

As a steering committee for the IMF, the G-20 countries have approximately 63 percent of the current voting power in the IMF and almost 80 percent of the voting power when including all the votes in the constituencies of which they are members. If EU representation in the G-20 were collapsed into one membership, that should further improve the effectiveness of the group and either contract its size to a G-16 or permit a slight expansion to 18.[32]

Paul Martin (2005) has called for an L-20—a G-20 at the leadership level of prime ministers and presidents—that builds on the finance group that already exists.[33] The G-20 group of countries is not without challenge as the steering committee for the global financial system. Peter B. Kenen et al. (2004) call for the creation of two new groups: (1) a G-4 involving the United States, the euro area, Japan, and China to coordinate exchange rate matters and (2) a Council for International Financial and Economic Cooperation (CIFEC) with 5 permanent and 15 term members. They argue that the CIFEC would have greater legitimacy, accountability, and representa-

---

31. Anyone can quibble about the G-20's membership on the margin, but it comes closer to meeting the test of including the systemically important countries than often is the case with political compromises.

32. David Peretz (2005) argues that the IMF needs an agenda-setting body of no more than 15 members that regularly meets at both the deputy and finance minister levels.

33. Martin's advocacy follows proposals by Colin Bradford and Johannes Linn (2004) and work by the Centre for Global Studies (2004).

tiveness than the existing finance G-20; their argument is not very per-suasive on the first two points given that the G-20 already exists, and on the third point any ad hoc group will be perceived by some nonpartici-pants as being nonrepresentative. They also propose that the CIFEC have a mandate to cover economic issues other than the IMF, which is also now the case for the G-7 and G-20.

More of a threat to the IMF as an institution, as well as to the G-20 as the steering committee for the international financial and monetary sys-tems that provides guidance for the IMF, would be the proposal by Kemal Derviş and Ceren Özer (2005) to create a new United Nations Economic and Social Security Council with six permanent and eight nonpermanent members who would exercise the votes of their constituencies. The votes would be an equally weighted combination of population, GDP, and con-tributions to the UN budget for global public goods. There would be no vetoes, but supermajorities would be required for some issues. The Coun-cil would (1) provide a strategic governance umbrella for international in-stitutions, including the IMF; (2) appoint the heads of those institutions, including the IMF, using transparent search procedures; and (3) mobilize resources for those institutions.

A similar but less well-developed idea is contained in the *Report of the Secretary-General's High-Level Panel on Threats, Challenges, and Change* (UN 2004). In part, these rival plans reflect turf battles between foreign min-istries and finance ministries; each ministry wants the institution in which it calls the shots to be dominant. In part, these plans reflect dissatisfaction with the orientation and governance of the Bretton Woods institutions.[34] It can also be argued that these proposals are intended to pull the Bretton Woods institutions into one common system for global governance.

The principal inference to be drawn from all this ferment with respect to a steering committee for the international financial system including the IMF is that in the immediate future that steering committee will not be drawn from the institutional structure of the IMF itself. If the choice is between the finance G-7 and G-20, it is difficult to imagine that the ratio-nal choice would not be the latter group appropriately reconfigured to in-clude only single representation of the European Union. However, that may not prove to be the choice. Political leaders have a sometimes dis-ruptive and counterproductive tendency to reach out to create new insti-tutions to address a renewed perception of recurrent global problems.

At the same time, political leaders frequently do respond to broader po-litical pressures—those manifested through NGOs at the national or in-

---

34. Dirk Messner et al. (2005) propose the creation of a Council for Global Development and Environment (CGDE) in the United Nations partly as a funding vehicle and also "with an enhanced mandate and sufficient legitimacy to counterbalance the independence of the Bret-ton Woods institutions from the UN System." The Fund and the World Bank are associated with the United Nations by mutual agreement, but they are not formally part of the UN Sys-tem of Organizations.

ternational level and those articulated by academics. This truth under-lines the challenge of communication that the Fund faces in today's world of instantaneous global transmission of information, misinformation, and disinformation: getting information out promptly about its programs and priorities. The institution has made important strides in communication and transparency over the past decade, but one has the sense that it has fallen further and further behind in the race to convey the truth about its policies, procedures, and accomplishments.

5

Lending Facilities

The traditional conception of IMF lending activities is that they should strike a balance between adjustment and financing. The borrowing country receives sufficient financing to allow it to take adjustment measures that minimize adverse effects on national or international prosperity. On its part, the country takes sufficient adjustment measures to ensure that it will be able to repay the Fund.[1]

As outlined in chapter 2, the IMF currently lends through five types of facilities: Stand-By Arrangements (SBA), an Extended Fund Facility (EFF), a Supplemental Reserve Facility (SRF), a Compensatory Financing Facility (CFF), and a Poverty Reduction and Growth Facility (PRGF).

In recent years there has been a trend toward streamlining the various facilities, revising them to reflect the changing realities of the international financial system—flexible exchange rates and more extensive private capital flows—and reducing their number in effect so that they can operate from one overall platform with multiple models or variations. For example, in the wake of the tsunami that hit Asian and African countries in December 2004, the Executive Board did not create a new facility; it approved an amendment to its "policy" on emergency lending to members in postconflict situations, which was adopted in 1995 and extended in 2001 to provide subsidized lending to countries that are PRGF eligible to include subsidized lending to countries hit by natural disasters. In March

---

1. This second half of the bargain is known as IMF "conditionality." It is frequently pointed out by critics of the IMF's operations today—for example, Bird (2003) and Babb and Buira (2005)—that the concept of conditionality is not to be found in the original IMF Articles of Agreement but was gradually insinuated into IMF policies, largely under the influence of the United States, which wanted to limit the size of IMF programs financed largely from its IMF quota. Conditionality was not codified until the 1969 amendment to the Articles of Agreement and was not supported by guidelines about how it was to be applied until the late 1970s.

2005, the Executive Board approved a Trade Integration Mechanism (TIM) as a policy associated with EFF or PRGF borrowing that permits countries to borrow to finance balance of payments shortfalls associated with multilateral trade liberalization.

Not all facilities involve actual lending. For example, the IMF long has had precautionary SBA or EFF lending arrangements under which the country has the right to borrow but states its intention not to do so. The underlying idea is that this type of program provides confidence to private-sector international lenders to the country by providing an IMF seal of approval of its policies. In the past, the Fund has also experimented with a variety of signaling devices and intensified monitoring mechanisms short of precautionary lending programs, and recent consideration has focused on a new type of nonborrowing program, a policy support instrument, that could be used by PRGF-eligible members; see the section on Support for Low-Income Countries.

Going the other way, from intentions not to borrow to promises to lend, in 1999 the IMF instituted a contingent credit line (CCL) feature into the SRF under which a specified amount of financing automatically became available to countries that had been preapproved to receive it. Despite tinkering with the feature, no one signed up for approval, and the CCL was not renewed in November 2003. However, as described below, variations on this general theme are under active discussion in the form of financial insurance for countries that have met preestablished conditions.

One fundamental issue is the question of which countries are likely to borrow from the IMF in the future. Data underlying tables 2.3, 2.4, and 2.5 reveal that 136 countries of the current 184 country members of the IMF have borrowed from the IMF during the past 30-plus years; see table 5.1.[2] Three additional countries, for a total of 139 members or 76 percent of the total membership, have had one or more programs under which they did not borrow. The countries include 38 percent of the industrial countries and 81 percent of all other IMF members, including 91 percent for the 77 PRGF-eligible countries (note that I have not classified India in the last category).

It is reasonable to assume that none of the industrial countries in the classification used in this paper will need to borrow again from the IMF, and the same may hold for a handful of other countries that we can

---

2. Most of the countries listed in table 5.1 had formal IMF programs; a few may have borrowed their first credit tranches, which do not require formal programs. The table does not include countries—for example, the United States—that only have borrowed all or part of their reserve tranche subscriptions to their IMF quota, in effect, borrowing back their reserves. Many of the borrowing countries have been "prolonged users" of IMF resources through successive borrowing programs. Sometimes such prolonged use may be appropriate, but it also raises questions about IMF program design, policies, and incentives. The IMF has acted in recent years to adopt new policies to take a closer look at and exert constraints on the phenomenon of prolonged use of IMF resources.

Table 5.1 Countries borrowing from the IMF, 1970–2005[a]

Category of countries	Borrowers (139)[b]	Nonborrowers (45)	Percent of borrowers (76)
Industrial countries (24)	Australia, Finland, Greece, Iceland, Italy, New Zealand, Portugal, Spain, United Kingdom (9)	Austria, Belgium, Canada, Denmark, France, Germany, Ireland, Japan, Luxembourg, Netherlands, Norway, San Marino, Sweden, Switzerland, United States (15)	38
Emerging-market countries (22)	Argentina, Brazil, Chile, China, Colombia, Czech Republic, Ecuador, Egypt, Hungary, India, Indonesia, Korea, Malaysia, Mexico, Philippines, Poland, Russian Federation, South Africa, Thailand, Turkey, Venezuela (21)	Singapore (1)	95
Other developing countries (61)	Algeria, Barbados, Belarus, Belize, Bosnia and Herzegovina, Bulgaria, Costa Rica, Croatia, Cyprus, Dominican Republic, El Salvador, Equatorial Guinea, Estonia, Fiji, Gabon, Guatemala, Iraq, Israel, Jamaica, Jordan, Kazakhstan, Latvia, Lithuania, Macedonia, Mauritius, Morocco, Panama, Paraguay, Peru, Romania, Serbia and Montenegro, Slovak Republic, Slovenia, St. Kitts and Nevis, Swaziland, Trinidad and Tobago, Tunisia, Ukraine, Uruguay (39)	Antigua and Barbuda, Bahamas, Kingdom of Bahrain, Brunei Darussalam, Botswana, Iran, Kuwait, Lebanon, Libya, Malta, Marshall Islands, Micronesia, Namibia, Oman, Palau, Qatar, Saudi Arabia, Seychelles, Suriname, Syrian Arab Republic, Turkmenistan, United Arab Emirates (22)	64
PRGF-eligible countries (77)	Afghanistan, Albania, Armenia, Azerbaijan, Bangladesh, Benin, Bolivia, Burkina Faso, Burundi, Cambodia, Cameroon, Cape Verde, Central African Republic, Chad, Comoros, Democratic Republic of Congo, Republic of Congo, Côte d'Ivoire, Djibouti, Dominica, Ethiopia, The Gambia, Georgia, Ghana, Grenada, Guinea, Guinea-Bissau, Guyana, Haiti, Honduras, Kenya, Kyrgyz Republic, Laos, Lesotho, Liberia, Madagascar, Malawi, Maldives, Mali, Mauritania, Moldova, Mongolia, Mozambique, Myanmar, Nepal, Nicaragua, Niger, Nigeria, Pakistan, Papua New Guinea, Rwanda, Samoa, São Tomé and Principe, Senegal, Sierra Leone, Solomon Islands, Somalia, Sri Lanka, Tanzania, Togo, Uganda, Uzbekistan, Vietnam, Yemen, Zambia, Zimbabwe (70)	Angola, Bhutan, Eritrea, Kiribati, Timor-Leste, Tonga, Vanuatu (7)	91

PRGF = Poverty Reduction and Growth Facility

a. The countries borrowing during 1970–75 are approximated on the basis of countries that had credit outstanding in 1975.

b. Colombia, Nigeria, and Paraguay have had IMF program(s) but have not borrowed.

Sources: IMF, *International Financial Statistics* (various years); IMF, annual reports (various years).

assume have continuous access to international capital markets or are so wealthy that they do not need it. Note that these countries, by assumption, face no international pressures to adjust, with the United States a leading example. However, approximately 75 percent of the IMF's membership, about 135 countries, are potential borrowers either because their access to international capital markets is subject to interruption or because they have little or no such access.

As noted in chapter 2, a number of potential borrowers from the IMF have taken steps in recent years to self-insure against the possible need to borrow external financial resources from the IMF by improving their macroeconomic policy frameworks, strengthening their financial systems, and building up their international reserves. However, the global economic environment has been remarkably benign over the past few years, with near record global growth, low inflation, strong commodity prices, and a sustained period of abnormally low nominal and real interest rates in the United States, the euro area, and Japan. These conditions will not persist. As Goldstein (2005b) details, the evidence is ample that a significant number of emerging-market countries could experience financial crises over the next five years because, in part, their self-insuring has been incomplete. For example, for many countries, sovereign and external debt levels remain unsustainable, and the benign global economic conditions could become less benign in a hurry.

The question is not only which countries will want to borrow from the IMF in the context of the next global economic downturn or period of adjustment of macroeconomic imbalances but also which countries should be eligible to borrow from the IMF. For some observers and critics, the answer to the second question is linked to the quality of IMF surveillance; effective surveillance in a crisis-prevention mode should lead to a reduced need to borrow. At the extreme, a smaller number of observers and critics would limit borrowing from the IMF to those countries that had previously received good report cards from the Fund. The report cards might contain a short list of subjects or a very long list of subjects.

The view that the scope of borrowing from the Fund should be and can be sharply reduced flies in the face of two realities. The IMF is an organization with a near universal global membership; those members are not going to leave other injured members, whether their injuries are self-inflicted or not, by the side of the road for the vultures to feed upon as carrion. Reinforcing this first reality is a second in the fact, persuasively argued by Daniel Tarullo (2005), that the IMF is a political institution established by governments that must respond to political forces, including forces of financial need. This reality, in his view, is fully consistent with the professionalism of the staff and the dedication of the management and shareholders to the global public good.

Therefore, we can reasonably expect a pickup in borrowing from the IMF during the next five years. What will be the content of the adjustment programs—the associated conditionality? At an abstract level, the policy conditions associated with borrowing from the IMF should be tailored to the nature and the origins of the shocks, disturbances, or policy miscalculations that give rise to the need to borrow from the Fund. For the 13 countries that have experienced financial crises, from Mexico in 1994 to Brazil in 2002, the range of economic and financial conditions prior to the crises is large (Roubini and Setser 2004, 28–29).[3] If only two country-specific dimensions—sovereign debt and external positions—are considered, Mexico (1994) and Thailand (1996) had large current account deficits and small stocks of sovereign debt—external plus internal. Russia (1997) had a large stock of sovereign debt and a current account surplus. Ecuador (1998) had a large current account deficit and a large stock of sovereign debt. To these two dimensions could be added currency mismatches, the exchange rate regime, the condition of the financial system, and many more. Global economic and financial conditions provide an additional overlay.

Critics from developing countries, for example, Buira (2003), observe that the principal IMF response to the myriad of circumstances that may contribute to a country's need to seek IMF financial support has been a complex elaboration of conditions on borrowing with a bias toward prompt external adjustment combined with limited financing built on optimistic assumptions about the restoration of access to financing from global financial markets.

In partial response to the first criticism about an excess of policy conditions, the IMF in 2002 adopted revised conditionality guidelines that emphasize country ownership of policies, parsimony in conditions, policies tailored to circumstances, appropriate coordination with other multilateral institutions, and clarity in the conditions themselves (IMF 2005i). Notwithstanding well-intentioned efforts to limit the scope of conditionality, each country's program in the end is different because its economic and financial circumstances differ, and the setting of policy conditions requires judgments, which means relying on discretion rather than rigid rules.

On the other side, critics argue that current practice results in "insufficient ambition" in IMF prescriptions for economic policy changes and reforms; IMF staff and management rely too heavily on the preferences and judgments of the national authorities.[4] Almost all observers agree that the fundamental challenge lies in determining what changes in policies will be effective in addressing a country's specific needs. Too little research has addressed this complex and vexing issue. However, it is clear that simple

---

3. The full list of countries is Mexico, Thailand, Indonesia, Korea, Malaysia, Russia, Brazil, Ecuador, Pakistan, Ukraine, Turkey, Argentina, and Uruguay.

4. Timothy Geithner remarked on this before the Bretton Woods Committee on June 10, 2004.

rules, for example, "it is mostly fiscal," do not do the trick. Moreover, it has yet to be established, but nevertheless is highly improbable in my view, that simple tests of degrees of ownership (political commitment to programs) or of the strength of institutions can explain much of the variance in policy performance under IMF programs.

The second criticism—the limited scale of financing based on false assumptions about the restoration of market access—challenges the hypothesis of the catalytic role of IMF programs: a strong economic program with its policy content endorsed by the IMF, even if the actual size of the Fund's financial support is small, will be associated with a prompt recovery of market access. Careful theoretical and empirical examinations of this hypothesis (Cottarelli and Giannini 2002; Mody and Saravia 2003) support the conclusion that the catalytic effects of IMF programs are limited. One important reason is that each country's case tends to be different, if not unique.

If the IMF cannot rely on the catalytic effects of its modest financial support for a country's program of economic adjustment, what should be the scale of IMF lending to countries? Answers to this question are usually couched in terms of a country's IMF quota, but such responses are complicated by inconsistencies in the size of countries' IMF quotas relative to their economic and financial development, as noted in chapter 4 on IMF governance. Answers are further complicated in the face of capital account crises, which are associated with a cessation or reversal of access to international capital markets by a country's borrowers in the public sector, private sector, or both.[5]

If a country faces an illiquidity crisis, which is often difficult to distinguish ex ante from an insolvency crisis, it is likely that its IMF program will have to be overfinanced ex ante if the country is to emerge from its crisis with a minimum of adverse economic and financial effects on that country and on the international financial system. Some would qualify this last statement and argue that the country can always declare a standstill on its external financial payments via capital controls and exchange restrictions. In recent years, no country has resorted to such extreme measures on a comprehensive basis in the context of a liquidity crisis.[6] Comprehensive controls were used in the Argentine case in 2001 and 2002 when it turned into a solvency crisis, but on the basis of that case it is questionable whether the standstill option would meet the test of minimizing economic and financial effects on a country in a liquidity crisis.

---

5. The cessation or reversal of capital inflows (a "sudden stop," as described by Calvo 1998) can be associated with latent or actual developments in internal policies, the external economic and financial environment, or both.

6. The Korean case and the Brazilian case are examples of limited exercises in this direction. Roubini and Setser (2004) advocate greater use of such tools.

The IMF has long had a policy of limiting a member's access to borrowing from the Fund to 100 percent of quota for one year and 300 percent of quota in total, but the Fund could approve exceptions. In recent years, with the advent of capital account crises, exceptional access has been approved in a small number of cases.[7] Those cases have been controversial within the Fund, among its members, and in the views of outside observers. In response, the IMF in 2002 and 2003 adopted and revised an exceptional access framework (EAF) that established certain analytical and procedural presumptions that should be applied to these cases.[8] Some (Goldstein 2005a; Roubini and Setser 2004) question the IMF's conscientiousness in applying this policy.

It is important not to exaggerate the relevance of exceptional access to IMF lending overall. Since 1994 only nine members of the IMF have been granted such access, albeit a number of them on several occasions. As of July 28, 2005, only 3 of the 14 current SBAs and EFFs involved exceptional access, those for Argentina, Turkey, and Uruguay. Only two other countries that previously had exceptional access to IMF resources had IMF credit outstanding on May 31, 2005: Brazil and Indonesia. Fourteen other emerging-market and developing countries had credit outstanding to the IMF as of that date. Korea, Mexico, Russia, and Thailand had repaid the IMF.

On the other hand, when the Executive Board approves exceptional access, the resulting program potentially ties up a substantial amount of the IMF's lending capacity because of the size of the programs. Some would argue that this situation argues for an expansion of IMF financial resources; others counter that doing so would increase inappropriately the number of programs with exceptional access. This subject is considered in more detail in the next section of this chapter.

---

7. One response to the capital account crises of the 1990s was to create the SRF under which countries can borrow larger amounts for shorter maturities at higher interest rates. These interest rate surcharges were later generalized in two forms: (1) the level of borrowing and (2) the time period covered by the borrowing. Surcharges now apply to EFF and CFF borrowing as well as SRF borrowing. Their interaction is complicated, and they have given rise to concerns about, and presumptive evidence of, arbitrage across facilities (IMF 2005b).

8. The analytical presumptions are (1) exceptional balance of payments pressures normally associated with a capital account crisis, (2) a rigorous analysis demonstrating debt sustainability, (3) a strong presumption of an early return to the capital markets, and (4) a strong program of policy adjustment accompanied by the political and institutional capacity to implement the program. The procedural presumptions are (1) an elevated burden of proof on IMF management and staff in presenting the recommended program, (2) early consultation with the Executive Board as the program is developed, and (3) required ex post evaluation of the program within a year after its end (IMF 2003). These elements have subsequently been tweaked somewhat in their application, but the basic framework remains as described. The framework is to be applied to IMF programs that involve exceeding the normal access limits of 100 percent of quota per year and total outstanding credit from the Fund of more than 300 percent of quota.

This introductory discussion of IMF facilities suggests the following basic questions: What should be the role of the IMF as an international lender? Should the IMF develop special programs to assist developing countries that are not experiencing financial crises but have large sovereign debts? Should special lending programs be developed for countries that are "good performers" as part of the array of IMF facilities or as the IMF's only facility? To what extent should the IMF offer or promote nonborrowing programs of policy support without financing? Should the IMF continue to offer special borrowing arrangements for low-income countries? The balance of this chapter elaborates on some of these questions and provides some answers to them. It covers (1) the IMF's role as an international lender, (2) in particular, its role with respect to members with large sovereign debts, (3) its lending to good performers, (4) programs of IMF support without the use of IMF financial resources, and (5) IMF programs with its low-income members.

The IMF as an International Lender

This is not the place to review the voluminous literature on the role of the IMF as an international lender to countries and whether it should be a lender of first, last, final, or highly limited resort. A sample of three recent contributions with differing views is Roubini and Setser (2004), Bedford, Penalver, and Salmon (2005), and ECB (2005).[9] The debate, which appears to be far from over, revolves around three issues: (1) limits on access to IMF financial resources, (2) private-sector involvement in the financing, and (3) the IMF's role in debt restructurings. A background issue is the changing nature of international financial markets, making international credit more available to some countries, but not necessarily on a continuous basis.

With regard to access limits, one central issue involves distinguishing cases of illiquidity from cases of insolvency (in the special case of countries, which in fact cannot be subjected to bankruptcy proceedings or the functional equivalent) and deciding whether the IMF has a role to play in preventing the former type of cases from turning into the latter. Although improved debt sustainability analyses and a greater understanding of the insidious effects of currency mismatches have aided in distinguishing liquidity cases from solvency cases, no consensus exists about the scale of IMF lending in such circumstances. Some favor strict absolute limits on IMF lending regardless of the circumstances, others favor constrained discretion close to if not identical with the current EAF, and still others see little merit in any limits.

---

9. IMF staff have been active contributors to this literature. See, for example, Giancarlo Corsetti, Bernardo Guimaraes, and Nouriel Roubini (2003), Olivier Jeanne and Charles Wyplosz (2001), Olivier Jeanne and Jeromin Zettelmeyer (2002), and Steven Morris and Hyun Song Shin (2003).

To the extent that one favors large-scale (exceptional access) lending by the IMF in reasonably well-defined circumstances, the analytical issues that the advocate must address are whether doing so involves an unacceptable increase in moral hazard with respect to the debtor or the creditors and whether more IMF lending improves a country's longer-term prospects by addressing the immediate problem or worsens them by piling up more debt (Rajan 2005b).

On the moral hazard issue, most observers agree that debtor moral hazard, while a theoretical possibility, is not a serious problem in light of the short-term political consequences of most crises.[10] On creditor moral hazard, again few disagree with the theoretical possibility, and many argue that it could be a serious issue. Olivier Jeanne and Jeromin Zettelmeyer (2004) construct a model that demonstrates that IMF lending creates no moral hazard as long as the Fund lends at actuarially fair interest rates and the borrowing country seeks to maximize the welfare of its taxpayers. Supporters of the moral hazard view of IMF lending must challenge these assumptions. However, within the context of the Jeanne-Zettelmeyer model, IMF lending may lead to large capital flows and better terms. Disagreement remains with respect to interpreting the empirical evidence associated with IMF lending over the past decade.[11] Even if one accepts that there is concrete evidence of a moral hazard effect of IMF lending, has that moral hazard created a serious distortion to international lending in the direction of favoring such lending to developing countries in the context of many other distortions? That is the crux of the issue.

At the abstract level of ex ante IMF policy, few would disagree with the characterization offered by Managing Director de Rato early in his term and since then often repeated: "[W]e clearly also need a Fund that can say 'No' selectively, perhaps more assertively, and, above all, more predictably than has been the case in the past."[12] What is notable about this statement is not its clarity but the qualifications: selectively, more assertively, and more predictably. De Rato's view does not differ substantially from that of his predecessor Horst Köhler (Camdessus, de Larosière, and Köhler 2004):

> The IMF is not a lender of last resort in the traditional sense; it isn't capable of providing an unlimited amount of financing. Once a crisis hits, the IMF needs to be

---

10. A more reasonable concern is the risk of supporting programs that are too timid in their policy content or may not be adequately implemented, contributing to further crises.

11. Jeanne and Zettelmeyer (2004, 15) survey the empirical literature and conclude: "Without exception, the tests performed in this literature are incapable of distinguishing whether the effects of the IMF on market variables (to the extent that any are found) are a sign of moral hazard or simply an indication that the IMF is doing its job."

12. Managing Director de Rato made these remarks in a speech, "The IMF at 60—Evolving Challenges, Evolving Role," at the IMF/Bank of Spain conference, Dollars, Debt and Deficits—60 Years after Bretton Woods, on June 14, 2004.

able to act quickly, and its involvement must be predictable to ensure that the private sector can play its part.[13]

How should the IMF strike the balance? Goldstein (2005a, 399–400) would move the pendulum further toward making it more difficult for the IMF to say yes. He would amend the Articles of Agreement to require supermajorities to approve exceptional access. He would also amend the Articles to require the managing director to sign off "explicitly" that any decision to grant exceptional access meets the requirements of the IMF's policy; at present there is only a strong presumption that any decision submitted to the Executive Board by IMF management is consistent with the IMF's conditionality guidelines and other policies, including access policy. Not only Rajan (2005b) but also Babb and Buira (2005) surprisingly favor tighter rules and less discretion. Rajan believes that discretion favors the borrower, and Babb and Buira believe that the borrower tends to be disfavored.

The relation between IMF lending and private-sector creditors during crises has been controversial at least since the 1980s. Contrary to the conventional wisdom, this is an area of evolution not revolution. Thus, Jacques de Larosière (Camdessus, de Larosière, and Köhler 2004) opines:

> The IMF cannot, and should not, provide all the financing for balance of payments problems; it has to count on private flows to do the bulk of the financing (heavy lending by the IMF to a few countries has become a serious issue for the institution and the system). Moreover, the IMF must develop a close relationship with the private sector and not turn a blind eye to it. . . . This was the rule in the 1980s. It still should be.

Roubini and Setser (2004) propose a comprehensive framework to address the role of the IMF during financial crises, the scale of its lending, and the participation of private-sector creditors: (1) distinguish promptly between liquidity and solvency situations, (2) adopt appropriate adjustment measures to match external financing with the nature of the crisis, (3) use large-scale IMF financing in a variety of circumstances, including in conjunction with coercive debt restructurings as necessary, (4) avoid the trap of countries (for example, Russia and Turkey) that are too strategic to fail, and (5) recognize that the IMF has a central coordinating role in the management of crises. Roubini and Setser recommend that the IMF create a crisis lending facility with lending limits of 300 percent of quota for one year and total lending of 500 percent of quota, which they regard as more realistic than the traditional limits of 100 and 300 percent of quota. However, they would allow these limits to be overridden with prespecified criteria.

---

13. Recall that Summers in a 1999 speech at the London School of Business also argued that the IMF has to be selective in providing its financial support.

The ECB (2005) task force favors the "effective" use and "predictable" commitment of all parties in debt crises (sovereign debtor, creditors, IMF, and creditor governments) to use available instruments (bond exchanges, rollover agreements, standstills, and, with less effect, capital controls and private contingent credit lines), with domestic creditors also bearing a part of the burden. They conclude from their review that crisis management practices have largely followed a case-by-case approach. In somewhat of a contradiction, they nevertheless favor efforts to improve the predictability of the process, including by reinforcing good relations between a debtor country and its creditors according to the "Principles for Stable Capital Flows and Fair Debt Restructuring in Emerging Markets" (also known as the code of conduct) that first was agreed to in the fall of 2004 between a group of emerging-market countries and a group of representatives of private-sector creditors; a slightly revised version was issued in March 2005. The principles cover transparency and information flows, continuous debtor-creditor dialogue, good faith actions by debtors and creditors, and fair treatment.[14]

The central banks of Canada and England with support from a number of other commentators and institutions in the past have favored absolute limits on access to IMF financing in conjunction with standstills on debt repayments as the appropriate mechanism to deal with external financial crises and the issues of moral hazard and predictability.[15] Bedford, Penalver, and Salmon (2005), commenting more recently in a Bank of England publication, place greater emphasis on market-based mechanisms for facilitating sovereign debt restructurings with further improvements in bond contracts beyond the widespread adoption of collective action clauses (CACs) and wider adoption of the code of conduct. They also favor more rigorous and informed application of the IMF's framework for exceptional access to IMF financial resources and a review of the IMF's policy on lending into arrears (LIA), when a member country has arrears to external private-sector creditors. With respect to LIA, they want the IMF to

---

14. The IMF (2005f, 14) asserts that the draft principles in the code of conduct "are broadly consistent with many of the expectations from Fund policies aimed at the prevention and resolution of financial crises." Among the identified exceptions are (a) linking continuation of trade and interbank lines to continued debt service by the sovereign debtor, (b) requiring the debtor to engage with a creditor committee, (c) the absence of consideration of voluntary standstills on litigation, (d) the resumption of partial debt service as a sign of good faith on the part of the borrower, and (e) the presumption that if a country's sovereign debt to the private sector is sought to be restructured the debtor must at the same time seek to restructure debt with all bilateral official creditors (reversing Paris Club comparability). The same document (IMF 2005f, 16) welcomes the code of conduct but dryly observes that "many market participants were not aware" of the code or principles and others argued that it was yet to be tested and lacked precision on a number of points.

15. Although the two central banks have not formally adopted policy positions on these issues, their leaders have tacitly endorsed the approach espoused by Andrew Haldane and Mark Kruger (2001), two senior members of their respective staffs.

publish its debt sustainability analysis but not to specify the financial parameters of its program until the debtor has reached agreement on them with its private-sector creditors. If the IMF were to adopt this last proposal, it would amount to a partial reversion to its policy in the early 1980s when programs were not approved by the IMF until a critical mass of creditors had agreed to the financing presumptions in the program, which at that time were initially agreed between the country and the IMF.[16]

A more radical change advocated by some (mostly IMF bashers on the right) in the context of the Argentine case would be to eliminate the IMF's de facto preferred creditor status—the presumption that the IMF will be paid in full even as other creditors are not. This would not only fly in the face of the logic of the IMF as a lender of final resort but also would effectively kill political support for the IMF in many industrial countries, as some advocates of such a position would like.

Note also that many of the proposed approaches to countries' external financial crises presume that those crises principally involve sovereign debt issued under international law, for example, the IMF's proposed Sovereign Debt Restructuring Mechanism (SDRM). This has been the exception rather than the rule. Of the 13 major country cases through 2002, only Argentina principally involved sovereign debt, as well as, possibly, the contagion case of Uruguay. Moreover, by the time 76 percent of the designated portion of Argentina's sovereign debt was restructured in mid-2005, domestic law governed more than half of its sovereign debt de facto or de jure. I wrote (Truman 2001), immediately after the SDRM proposal was initially floated, that the proposal was too much (for the international financial system to accept at the time) and too little (it might be useful in a few cases, but only on the margin). My forecast was unusually accurate. The SDRM was cut back and put on the shelf. It did vastly accelerate the adoption and acceptance of CACs.

The Argentine case, of course, ultimately involved a sovereign default; widespread defaults on private-sector obligations to foreign and domestic creditors (including banks); a collapse of the domestic banking system; and restrictions on capital flows, domestic access to foreign exchange, and access to bank deposits. Thus, in reconsidering the appropriate role of the IMF as an international lender in this context, one should also reconsider the IMF role in crisis prevention with respect to balance sheet mismatches, the appropriateness of capital controls at least in crisis prevention, and other approaches to modulate booms and busts in international lending.

Finally, the IMF's role as an international lender is linked to its role in restructuring situations. If the IMF determines before or after a crisis

---

16. That practice was changed in 1989 to one of IMF lending into arrears to banks because over time the previous policy of requiring a "critical mass" of private-sector support was regarded as giving the creditor banks too much leverage in the context where the debtors generally were meeting their obligations. The IMF's LIA policy was extended in 1998 to bondholders.

breaks that a country faces a solvency crisis, the Roubini-Setser approach would call for a debt restructuring, perhaps a coercive restructuring accompanied by IMF lending to ease the burden on the country.[17] We have already seen that Bedford, Penalver, and Salmon (2005) want the IMF to stay out of the way and let "market mechanisms" operate.

In my view, the flaw in arguments that the IMF should not interfere with the market is that in crisis or near-crisis situations market mechanisms will likely break down, and the system does not have a natural replacement to play a coordinating role. Collective action clauses in sovereign bond contracts governed by international law are not a substitute where a large proportion of the debt does not take that form. Even where international bonds dominate, clauses promoting intercreditor coordination can be expected to have a limited impact because they do little to alter the leverage between the debtor and the creditors as a group. Once the debtor has defaulted, the creditors have essentially no leverage to force action. In the Argentine case, where the stakes were high, legal efforts have so far failed (Gelpern 2005).

It follows that it is reasonable for the IMF, as a collective institution, to address this market failure by playing a coordinating role. This is the view of Roubini and Setser (2004), and I fully agree with them. The resulting restructuring inevitably will have a political dimension, which is not surprising since one of the parties is a government and because of the necessarily political foundations of the IMF (Tarullo 2005). Moreover, one cannot duck the fact that the IMF has a financial interest in the outcome even if it has de facto status as a preferred creditor.[18] The issue is whether the alternative to the former traditional procedures would produce superior outcomes. I have my doubts.

In the case of Argentina after 2001, the IMF at Argentina's insistence but with the general support and often the vigorous encouragement of the G-7 countries abandoned its practice of more than 25 years of acting as a coordinator and umpire in debt settlements. That practice evolved during the debt crises of the 1980s, when Jacques de Larosière led the IMF, through the capital account crises of the 1990s, when Michel Camdessus was its leader.[19] In contrast, Argentina's 2003 IMF program did not establish any parameters for the country's offer to its bondholders—an omis-

---

17. Roubini and Setser (2004) do not exclude standstills, rollovers, or restructurings in the case of liquidity crises, with the IMF playing a coordinating role.

18. As noted earlier, many critics of the IMF call for the abandonment of its preferred creditor status. Roubini and Setser (2004, 253–54) successfully demolish their arguments.

19. IMF policy was not perfectly suited to every case, but it evolved. Some argue that the slow evolution of the 1980s and the delayed establishment of the policy of lending into arrears prolonged the debt crises of that period, which were global and not limited to Latin America. My view from the trenches was that the responsible officials of few countries wanted debt reduction much before it was on offer in the Brady Plan in 1989.

sion that Argentina exploited. Only belatedly did IMF management and the G-7 articulate a verbal formula describing a successful restructuring. It was defined as a restructuring that was "sustainable" and "comprehensive." Since the restructuring left Argentina with a public-sector debt ratio of more than 75 percent of GDP, one can doubt whether the result is sustainable. Since 24 percent of the relevant debt was not treated, it is certainly not comprehensive. By its own criteria, the IMF's noninvolvement produced a failure. Argentina may have failed as well. The perception is that greater IMF involvement would have provided a better deal for bondholders. In fact, IMF involvement might have produced an endorsement of deeper debt reduction.

Could the IMF have played a more forceful role? Of course it could have done so even though the Argentine government expressed no interest in the IMF playing such a role. The IMF was bluffed into supporting Argentina's economic program and effectively a partial rollover of Argentine obligations to the IMF. The Fund and its larger members had a choice. They failed to insist upon either of the two related conditions that Timothy Geithner in remarks before the Bretton Woods Committee on June 10, 2004, recommended in such situations: a credible medium-term adjustment program and a credible and monitorable framework for achieving a viable debt restructuring.

Notwithstanding these criticisms, many have applauded the IMF's non-role in the Argentine debt restructuring. The US government was a leading supporter of that posture. To date, US government officials have expressed no regrets, although Randal Quarles (2005) both praised the progress to date and argued that more work needs to be done with respect to the residual defaulted debt. Allan Meltzer, in testimony on June 7, 2005, before the Subcommittee on International Trade and Finance of the US Senate Committee on Banking, Housing and Urban Affairs on the subject of IMF reform, praised the IMF for its noninvolvement and argued that its policy was "a big step forward." Reuters reported on July 29, 2005, that Managing Director de Rato insisted that the Fund should have no role in the negotiations between the Argentine government and its creditors. One can only speculate how de Rato is going to square his statement with the view that Argentina must have a strategy to deal with the remainder of its defaulted debt as part of any new IMF program. The IMF played a much more active role in the rescheduling of the external debts of the Dominican Republic in 2004; perhaps it has begun to learn its lessons.

Only time will tell about many aspects of the Argentine case. To date the largest sovereign debt default in history has passed without definitively answering any legal and policy questions surrounding it (Gelpern 2005). Argentina has faced rather limited legal consequences from its default and its bond exchange. Gelpern sees the associated documentation as progressive, not revolutionary. The next act in this debt drama again involves Argentina and the IMF despite the IMF's posture to date of noninvolvement.

Will the IMF management and a majority of its members once again blink and approve a program with Argentina without a plan to achieve comprehensive and sustainable settlement of its defaulted debt? If the answer is yes, this will only reinforce the principal conclusion so far from this sorry experience: Once a country has defaulted, the country—not its creditors—has most of the leverage. As a result of its noninvolvement posture, the IMF effectively allowed itself to be manipulated by the defaulting country into a posture perceived as against the country's creditors without articulating its position. This result, if it stands, will not enhance the stature of the IMF as part of the international financial architecture.

Support for Members with Large Debts

Countries that successfully emerge from financial crises and IMF programs with large stocks of sovereign debt (internal and/or external) and countries with large stocks of sovereign debt, for example, above 30 percent of GDP, that have not experienced financial crisis are particularly vulnerable to internal and external shocks that precipitate a crisis or another crisis. What should the IMF role be with respect to such countries?

One alternative is to monitor the countries and their performance via Article IV consultations, coaxing and cajoling them to adopt policies that place debt ratios on a convincing downtrend. Those countries that have emerged from a crisis might face a higher-than-normal bar as they seek to obtain additional IMF financial support at least until they have paid down a substantial fraction of their earlier IMF loans. Those countries that have yet to face crises would be dealt with the same way as the first group of countries, except that the bar to IMF lending might be lower.

At the other extreme, following Roubini and Setser (2004), the IMF could actively encourage and financially support debt restructurings that promise significant reductions in debt stock. Such preemptive restructuring would be difficult to sell to the market, but the long-run benefits to the countries might well offset the short-term costs. In effect, this was the approach attempted under the Brady Plan restructurings of commercial bank debt in the early 1990s.[20]

An intermediate alternative has been suggested by Derviş and Özer (2005): establishment in the IMF, in cooperation with the World Bank, of a Stability and Growth Facility (SGF) to help emerging-market economies with strong economic policies and large sovereign debt ratios achieve sustainable growth as they work down their debt ratios and to protect them

---

20. The Brady restructurings resulted in limited if any reductions in debt stocks as valued by the market at the time, but the gap between face value and market value was recognized, and repayments were reprogrammed.

from financial crises unrelated to their current economic policies. In effect, the IMF would provide financing against external debt shocks, creating demand for a bigger IMF.

Derviş and Özer suggest that countries such as Brazil, Ecuador, Indonesia, the Philippines, Turkey, and Uruguay might now qualify as long as their policies were judged ex ante to be strong enough. The proposal involves elements of both prequalification in terms of economic policies and insurance against unforeseen shocks. In principle, it would allow countries that experience, for example, a sharp drop in exports because of a global economic slowdown to run countercyclical fiscal policies, or at least not procyclical fiscal policies, in the context of a decline in domestic economic activity.

Many questions would have to be answered before the establishment of such a facility. One important question would be the likely need for additional IMF financial resources and how those resources might be assembled, which is the topic of the next chapter.

IMF Lending Programs for Good Performers

The SGF proposal outlined above is one variant on a number of proposals that would involve prepositioning IMF lending programs for countries that are "good performers." It does not require much imagination to sketch out other variants on this theme.

The first set of questions in connection with such proposals involves the definition of good performance. What objective indicators would be used to establish good performance? Candidates might include fiscal positions, average marginal and effective tax rates, debt positions of the government and country, exchange rate regimes or performance, international reserves, inflation rates, and condition of financial sectors, to name a few possibilities. Identifying good performers could be linked to IMF Article IV consultations or other IMF surveillance activities. Countries could automatically qualify, or they could apply for certification. Recertifying and decertifying countries presumably would involve the same procedures, but how those procedures would operate and with what frequency are other important questions involving political issues as well as internal IMF bureaucratic issues.

A second set of questions involves the conditions or context in which access to the facility could be activated. Would they be prespecified and objective as well? This would imply that access would be essentially automatic. Alternatively, the Executive Board might be expected to review evidence assembled by the IMF staff and endorsed by the management before funds were released.

A third set of questions is whether the IMF should lend only to countries that had qualified by meeting a (large or small) set of conditions. The

IFIAC (2000) majority endorsed the IMF playing essentially a quasi lender of last resort exclusively to emerging-market economies that had met a short list of four preconditions (Williamson 2001): (1) freedom of entry and operation for foreign financial institutions; (2) well-capitalized commercial banks; (3) regular, timely, and comprehensive publication of the maturity structure of sovereign and guaranteed debt; and (4) an unspecified indicator of fiscal probity.[21] Nothing was included with respect to the size of sovereign debt stocks, current account deficits, exchange rate regimes, inflation rates, or a number of other variables many would consider relevant to economic and financial stability. C. Fred Bergsten, who was a dissenting member of the Meltzer Commission with respect to this issue, points out (in testimony before the Subcommittee on International Trade and Finance of the US Senate Committee on Banking, Housing and Urban Affairs on June 7, 2005) critically that the suggested criteria would have permitted continued IMF lending to Argentina in the summer of 2001 but would not have permitted the Fund to lend to Brazil in 2002. Goldstein (2003, 238–44) also presents a detailed critical analysis of the IFIAC proposal.

The CCL provided a country in principle with an opportunity to seek preapproved financial support and a limited amount of automatic access. However, even this modest step in the direction of an insurance facility was tightly circumscribed. Many influential members of the IMF, in particular many European members, opposed the concept because they wanted slower disbursements and stronger policy conditions. No IMF members chose to apply for a CCL. The result was that the CCL was not renewed in 2003.

However, the idea of some type of IMF insurance facility is not dead. Most of the new ideas differ from the CCL in that the CCL used an application mechanism, and under most of the insurance type of schemes countries would be prequalified without formally applying. Daniel Cohen and Richard Portes (2004) have made such a proposal. Tito Cordella and Eduardo Levy Yeyati (2005) have as well. Barry Eichengreen (2004) expresses support for an Enhanced Monitoring Facility that appears to be a cross between the CCL and a full-blown insurance facility. Rajan (2005a) can be interpreted as endorsing consideration of such a facility as part of an IMF move toward greater reliance on rules than discretion.

Ralph Chami, Sunil Sharma, and Ilhyock Shim (2004) analyze the theoretical case for an IMF coinsurance arrangement and find it lacking in the face of information asymmetries and time-consistency weaknesses. On the other hand, such flaws affect most other elements of macroeconomic policymaking, and policy is made nonetheless.

---

21. In extremis, a threat to the stability of the global financial system, the IFIAC said the IMF should be able to lend to other countries that had not prequalified.

At the more practical level, Timothy Geithner, in his remarks before the Bretton Woods Committee on June 10, 2004, laid out five key elements of a credible IMF insurance mechanism: (1) a policy framework that can be counted upon to restore confidence, (2) a scale of financing calibrated to need (potentially substantial), (3) flexibility to respond to external circumstances and the borrower's policy effort (implying scope for the front-loading of large amounts of financing), (4) use in the context of restructuring efforts, and (5) a more credible capacity for the IMF to withstand arrears in repayments. The Geithner elements clearly involve aspects of the IMF's operations that extend beyond relatively narrow issues of prequalification.

What are the prospects for a new effort in this area reaching fruition? UK finance minister Brown (2005) expressed some sympathy for the idea. His French counterpart, Breton (2005), supported it. The G-24 (2005) expressed cautious support for exploring the idea of a precautionary facility as long as it was adequately financed to deal with capital account crises. This is an idea whose time may not have come, but it is not dead either.

Support Without Lending

The IMF has long wrestled with the issue of how to support countries with strong or strengthening economic policies that do not need financial support or cannot afford financial support because of the financial cost of borrowing even from the IMF.[22] In effect, the IMF by approving such an arrangement would be providing a signal to the market or to other investors and donors. The IMF now has, and in the past has experimented with, similar instruments taking the form of (1) precautionary arrangements that permit a country to borrow even if borrowing is not expected,[23] (2) staff-monitored programs that involve no IMF resources and often have been used as precursors to regular programs, and (3) enhanced surveillance or monitoring by the staff or Executive Board sometimes in connection with programs that have recently ended.

One issue with respect to such mechanisms is how they should be linked with normal surveillance mechanisms, for example, Article IV consultations. Wouldn't the IMF become just another rating agency (Jack Boorman suggested this in remarks in London in November 2004), and what would be its value added? Another issue is whether the signal to the market or to other investors and donors tends to absolve those receiving the signal from doing their own due diligence—another type of moral haz-

---

22. See IMF (2004e) reporting on the Executive Board's discussion of this topic in September 2004 and related documents.

23. As of July 28, 2005, 3 of the 14 operational SBA or EFF arrangements were precautionary: those for Colombia, Croatia, and Paraguay. Often the proportion has been larger.

ard. A third issue involves the black-or-white character of off-on signals, when the true situation almost always involves shades of gray. A related very important issue is the implication of turning off a signal once it has been turned on. This, in turn, relates to the standards that are to be applied: Are the standards higher or lower for a regular standby arrangement or a precautionary standby arrangement or for a low-access arrangement even though the standards in the latter cases in principle are the same as in the former? Are standards in signaling mechanisms the same as those associated with upper-credit-tranche SBA and EFF arrangements or are they lower?

A final set of issues involves whether the signaling mechanism would be voluntary and whether it would be limited to one category of countries, for example, low-income countries or emerging-market countries, or would it be available for all categories of countries. If the use of the mechanism were voluntary, would there be any volunteers? How should their volunteering be interpreted?[24]

A special type of IMF support for a country, where only limited IMF resources would be involved, is a mechanism whereby the Fund provides an instrument to help a member cope with a negative external shock such as a drop in the price of a commodity that represents a large share of its export earnings by linking repayments to the IMF to an external index. The facility would assist the country to avoid procyclical fiscal policies.

Kristin Forbes (2005) has proposed such a mechanism for dealing with external shocks. Her proposal bears a family resemblance to the CFF, which provides countries a modest amount of access to IMF financing with low conditionality in the context of negative external shocks. The terms for access to the CFF have been tightened in recent years, which has contributed to sharply reduced use of the facility compared with the 1970s and early 1980s. Buira (2005a, 23–24) suggests that a more representative governance structure at the IMF might lead to a reversal of these trends.[25]

---

24. The answer to the first question appears to be yes. The Nigerian government indicated in the summer of 2005 its interest in utilizing such a mechanism as the basis for obtaining a write-down and rescheduling of its bilateral official debt. The Paris Club indicated its willingness to accept such a policy support instrument as the basis for such an agreement with Nigeria. The Paris Club press release of June 28, 2005, states that Nigeria would be receiving exceptional treatment in the interest of resolving Nigeria's long-standing arrears to Paris Club creditors. Normally, Paris Club agreements are predicated upon an IMF standby arrangement or the equivalent. We will see whether the exception becomes the rule. It is noteworthy in terms of the second question that Nigerian government officials have been quoted as saying that this form of IMF support will not involve conditions on Nigerian economic and financial policies.

25. It is of some note in connection with the CFF and related facilities that the G-8 finance ministers meeting in London on June 11, 2005, agreed that "the IFIs [international financial institutions] have a role in helping address the impact of higher oil prices on adversely affected developing countries and encourage the IMF to include oil prices in the development

At the IMFC meeting in April 2004, US Secretary of the Treasury Snow (2004) reopened IMF consideration of a mechanism (a policy monitoring arrangement) through which the IMF could provide support for members without lending:

> To strengthen its policy role, we favor the development of a new form of engagement for countries that do not have a financing need. Under this proposal, the IMF could assess an economic program prepared by the country itself and signal its view to donors, MDBs [multilateral development banks], and markets. Such a nonborrowing vehicle for close engagement would benefit both poor countries and emerging-market countries, as it will show that a country has clear ownership of its policies and is strong enough to stand on its own feet.

In April 2005, the G-7 and the IMFC indicated their support for the US proposal in the context of the IMF's engagement with low-income (PRGF-eligible) countries. Part of the rationale is that these countries cannot afford to borrow even on highly subsidized PRGF terms, and the proposed mechanism would be analogous to a grant of policy endorsement without financial resources.

At the April 2005 meeting of the IMFC, Germany's minister of finance, Hans Eichel (2005), indicated his support for the establishment of a policy-monitoring arrangement to assist countries in graduating from IMF financial support as long as the terms involved upper-credit-tranche conditionality and regular reviews by the Executive Board. The Canadian finance minister, Ralph Goodale (2005), also expressed support for the idea to strengthen surveillance relationships with developing countries in general, those with higher incomes as well as low incomes per capita.

Acting Under Secretary Quarles (2005) reported to the US Congress on progress in promoting the US initiative with respect to nonborrowing IMF programs. In his remarks, he left open the possibility that the mechanism would be available to all members of the IMF, not just to low-income members. Time will tell whether the mechanism will be generalized, but such a "policy support instrument" that does not involve IMF lending was put in place for low-income countries shortly after the 2005 IMF annual meetings.

Support for Low-Income Countries

IMF support for low-income countries, defined for these purposes as PRGF-eligible members, takes many forms.[26] They participate, of course,

---

of facilities to respond to shocks." In November 2005, the IMF Executive Board established such an exogenous shock facility for low-income members and the United Kingdom and several other governments announced they would help finance it.

26. In September 2004, Managing Director de Rato, in remarks on June 14, 2004, at the IMF/Bank of Spain conference, Dollars, Debt and Deficits, stressed the IMF's partnership role in supporting its low-income members.

directly and through their representatives in all IMF activities. They all are covered by IMF surveillance. They receive technical assistance from the IMF. By definition they are eligible to borrow from the PRGF and to receive related forms of highly subsidized financial support. In principle, they are also eligible to borrow from other facilities, including the CFF, the EFF, and regular SBA. Those low-income countries that are also in the category of Heavily Indebted Poor Countries (HIPC) have, since 1999, been potentially eligible for partial reduction of their debts to the IMF and other international financial institutions, and a subset of them are now expected to be in line for 100 percent reduction of their debts to the IMF.[27]

It was not always the case that low-income countries had special IMF facilities. In 1975, when 49 of the current 77 PRGF-eligible countries were members of the Fund, 28 of them had credit outstanding to them from the Fund on regular financial terms. For the most part, the absolute poverty of these countries was no lower in 1975 than it is today. At that time, the international community was less sensitive to the buildup of their external debts, more optimistic that low-income countries would be able to grow out of their debts, or more concerned that special facilities distorted the universal character of the Fund.

Another important change during the past 30 years has been the progressive shift of the IMF from balance of payments lending into longer-term, structural adjustment lending, which accelerated in the late 1980s (Bird 2003, 2–10). First, the IMF in 1975 established a Trust Fund with some of the proceeds from its gold sales for lending to low-income countries. In 1976 the EFF was created. In early 1986, a Structural Adjustment Facility (SAF) replaced and absorbed the Trust Fund. In 1987, the SAF was transformed into an Enhanced Structural Adjustment Facility (ESAF). However, "structural adjustment" had a bad ring to it. Moreover, the NGO community criticized the ESAF because, with some reason, it saw structural policy conditions being imposed on countries merely so that they could qualify for loans that were largely employed to refinance old loans from the IMF. Thus, the ESAF morphed into the PRGF where, in principle, the borrowing country through the participatory drafting of its PRSP has a greater say in the policy conditions. This process is described as an effort to improve ownership and performance. To some observers it is a manifestation of IMF and World Bank policy failure.

The transformation of the nature of IMF lending to low-income countries into structural lending, by one name or another, has meant that the IMF increasingly has become involved with policy issues that had been principally the responsibility of the World Bank. Similarly, the Bank has

---

27. The G-8 proposal for 100 percent reduction of debts of certain HIPC borrowers from the IMF has implications not only for those countries but also for the IMF's involvement with them and potentially for the IMF's financial structure because of the involvement of the IMF's gold. The IMF Executive Board reached agreement on this new "multilateral debt relief initiative" on November 7, 2005.

become more involved in and conscious of the macroeconomic and financial policies of countries receiving World Bank loans. Consequently, the Fund and the Bank have been called upon to collaborate more intensively and with mixed results.[28]

Three issues are on the agenda for IMF reform with respect to its support for low-income members: Should the IMF continue to lend to these members? Should the IMF's involvement in PRGF lending be terminated? If IMF participation in PRGF lending is terminated, what type of lending arrangements for low-income countries, if any, should take its place?

The Bush administration, aggressively following up on initiatives of the Clinton administration with respect to the development agenda for low-income countries (HIPC relief and greater reliance on grants), has included on its expanded agenda a number of elements involving the IMF's support of such countries. Secretary Snow (2004) at the April meeting of the IMFC advocated that (1) the IMF continue to lend to poor members but only for balance of payments needs; (2) development needs should be met by development banks and bilateral donors, not the IMF; (3) the IMF should marshal grants to support strong performers and those facing macroeconomic setbacks; and (4) low-income countries with strong fundamentals should move beyond PRGF borrowing to nonborrowing engagement with the IMF.

The US-supported elements are part of an ongoing debate about the IMF with respect to low-income members. The basic argument for continued intensive IMF involvement with its low-income members is that good macroeconomic policy is crucial to economic development, growth, and the reduction of poverty. The management and staff of the IMF are not inclined to back off from engagement with its low-income members. In their view, the IMF is the accepted international arbiter of such policies and must be continuously engaged in their support and evaluation. Furthermore, if the IMF is to play its role effectively, it needs to use its "own money" as leverage.

In April 2004, before the IMFC meeting, the Executive Board (IMF 2004b) expressed its continued support for the IMF's "important role in low-income member countries in terms of surveillance, policy advice, financing and technical assistance." Most directors preferred the continued availability of small PRGFs. Many directors did not support precautionary PRGF arrangements—an alternative to nonborrowing support.

The spring 2005 IMFC communiqué devoted five paragraphs exclusively to the IMF and its support for low-income countries, demonstrating little appetite to disengage from lending to low-income members. The

---

28. This collaboration and the issues that give rise to the need for it are not limited to the low-income countries. Structural issues are part of IMF-supported programs with most members, and the Bank since the 1980s has been—some would say excessively—conscious of the macroeconomic and financial context of lending to all of its borrowers.

French finance minister, Thierry Breton (2005), explicitly said that the existing PRGF is a suitable tool for the IMF as a universal institution to use to support low-income countries.

With respect to collaboration between the Fund and World Bank on country programs and conditionality, the IMF executive directors (IMF 2004c) concluded that the evidence supported renewed support for the existing operational framework for such collaboration. At the same time they stressed that there was no room for complacency with respect to country ownership and tensions over the coverage of conditionality and the scope and pace of reforms.[29]

All observers do not accept the status quo with respect to the IMF's role in the PRGF. Allan Meltzer, in testimony on June 7, 2005, before the Subcommittee on International Trade and Finance of the US Senate Committee on Banking, Housing and Urban Affairs, consistent with the majority recommendation of the 2000 report of the IFIAC that he chaired, stated simply that the PRGF should be closed. The Council on Foreign Relations (1999) report implied as much in its recommendation that the Fund and Bank should refocus on their respective core activities. C. Fred Bergsten, a member of the IFIAC, stated before the Subcommittee on International Trade and Finance of the US Senate Committee on Banking, Housing and Urban Affairs on June 7, 2005, that he would prefer to transfer the PRGF to the World Bank because the Bank's primary mission is poverty reduction. Nancy Birdsall and John Williamson (2002) recommend that the PRGF be transferred from the IMF to the World Bank to make the PRSP process the unambiguous responsibility of the Bank and to achieve some administrative savings. David Bevan (2005), commenting on a choice among (1) the status quo, (2) dropping the balance of payments facade associated with IMF lending to the low-income countries through the PRGF and adopting a more realistic IMF program of 25-year financial support, and (3) the IMF's getting out of the business of long-term loans, favors the third option. One wonders whether the prospect of 100 percent IMF debt reduction for a subset of the HIPC borrowers from the IMF under the PRGF will not and should not lead to a reassessment of this issue by the IMF's membership as a whole, leading to the third option.

If the PRGF were transferred to the World Bank, a question would remain whether the IMF should get completely out of the business of lending to low-income countries. Some say yes. Others argue that the possibility of lending to meet traditional, short-term, balance of payments needs should not be excluded. That appears to be the position of Canada's finance minister, Ralph Goodale (2005), who expressed support for limiting the PRGF to providing "rapid assistance to alleviate short-term external payments

---

29. The underlying document was based on a survey of Fund mission chiefs and Bank country directors. No doubt some of them were forthright in their responses, but one wonders whether there were not incentives to support the status quo.

distress" for low-income members of the IMF. This is a reasonable position, and such lending to very poor countries might also be subsidized.

What about ensuring sound macroeconomic policies in low-income countries? One approach would be that the IMF should continue to conduct its surveillance of the policies—macroeconomic and financial-sector policies—of its low-income members. The World Bank in its IDA lending should take account of the IMF's views. Where the Bank staff agrees with those views it should say so in its documentation and where it does not it should also explain its views. Continued Article IV consultations and ex post evaluations of IDA lending should over time induce more de facto coordination than occurs de jure today. The Bank would learn from its mistakes and pay for them. One problem some might reasonably argue is that the shareholders that would pay are also the shareholders in the IMF.

All of these issues are yet to be resolved.

6

Financial Resources

The IMF is an international financial institution. Like other financial institutions it is in the business of making loans consistent with its charter and policies, in other words, under appropriate circumstances and with appropriate conditions and protections. The determination of appropriate circumstances and appropriate conditions and protections is one place where selectivity enters the picture.[1] Appropriate conditions include the potential for private-sector involvement in financing a country in crisis.[2] A natural question is whether the IMF has enough financial resources to carry out its responsibilities now and for the immediate future.

If the answer to this first question is that it does not now have adequate resources to discharge its responsibilities or it is likely to run short over the next 5 to 10 years, then a follow-up question is how best should the IMF augment its resources? Should it look toward another increase in quotas? Should it rely more heavily on borrowing from members through standing arrangements such as the General Arrangements to Borrow (GAB) and the New Arrangements to Borrow (NAB) or through ad hoc means? Alternatively, should it look to borrow in the market or should it seek to mobilize the latent profits on its holdings of gold?

Finally, where do SDR fit into the IMF's activities and its financial operations in the 21st century? Is it important to ratify the Fourth Amendment of the Articles of Agreement?[3] Looking forward, should the SDR be put on

---

1. On circumstances and conditions, see also the discussion and information in chapter 2.

2. Selectivity also enters the picture with respect to crisis prevention, surveillance, and possible prequalification for IMF lending.

3. The Fourth Amendment provides a one-time allocation of SDR in order to put members of the IMF that joined after the first 1970–72 and/or second 1979–81 general allocations of SDR on a roughly equal footing with other members.

the shelf, should regular allocations be resumed, should existing allocations be cancelled, or should the mechanism be transformed so it can provide some type of global public good rather than just increasing global liquidity? This chapter examines (1) the IMF's need for additional resources, (2) how its resources should be augmented, and (3) the future role of the SDR.

The IMF's Need for More Resources

Does the IMF need more financial resources right away today or tomorrow? The answer is almost certainly no.

As of July 28, 2005, the IMF's one-year forward commitment capacity, the metric it now uses to measure its capacity to make new financial commitments, was about $133 billion, easily the highest level in its history and essentially twice its lending capacity at the end of 2002.[4] In addition, the IMF has another approximately $50 billion available from its standing borrowing arrangements, the GAB and the NAB. An alternative traditional measure of IMF lending capacity, the IMF's liquidity ratio, is 2¼ times what it was at the end of 2002.[5] This dramatic improvement reflects in part the repayments and early repayments to the Fund by Russia and Brazil and, in part, benign global economic and financial conditions that have meant that there have not been any large net new demands on the IMF.

Quotas are the traditional source of IMF resources to lend although borrowing from members from time to time has been used as a supplement, and the PRGF is financed by borrowing. The second memorandum item in table 2.4 provides the IMF's credit outstanding as a percentage of total quotas for seven dates during the past 30 years. The average is 26.6 percent, and the figure for May 31, 2005, was 26 percent. Table 6.1 provides a longer-term perspective on IMF quotas relative to a number of other indicators of the development of the global economy. I estimate that, as of the end of 2005, total IMF quotas relative to reserves will have fallen to the lowest level in the past 35 years; this reflects in large part the buildup in foreign exchange reserves by a large number of countries since the end of 2000. On the other hand, total IMF quotas relative to GDP at market prices are within the range of the past 30 years, and total quotas relative to international trade in goods and services are only slightly below their range over that period.[6]

---

4. The IMF defines its "one-year forward commitment capacity" as its usable resources (holding of currencies of members in strong enough external positions that their currencies can be lent to other countries plus the IMF's holdings of SDR) *minus* undrawn balances under lending commitments *plus* projected repayments to the Fund over the next year *minus* a generous prudential balance.

5. The liquidity ratio is the ratio of net uncommitted resources to liquid liabilities.

6. As is almost always the case, different calculations by different authors can suggest somewhat different conclusions. For a longer period, Buira (2005a) estimates that the size of the

Table 6.1   IMF quotas relative to reserves, GDP, and trade (percent)

Year	Foreign exchange reserves	GDP	International trade[a]
1970	62.2	0.83	7.1
1975	21.3	0.54	3.2
1980	20.3	0.65	3.2
1985	25.6	0.76	4.2
1990	14.8	0.57	3.0
1995	15.6	0.74	3.5
2000	14.1	0.87	3.5
2004	8.9	0.81	3.0
2005(e)[b]	7.0	0.71	2.6
2015(p)[c]	2.9	0.57	1.6

(e) = estimate
(p) = projection

a. Average of world exports and imports of goods and services.
b. Data for 2005 are estimated using the compound growth rates for 2000–04.
c. Projections for 2015 use the average of the compound growth rates for the periods 1990–95, 1995–2000, and 2000–04: foreign exchange reserves (11.5 percent); GDP (4.5 percent); and trade (7.2 percent). IMF quotas are projected for 2005 at their end-2004 level adjusted to the dollar/SDR rate on July 25, 2005. The 2015 projection assumes a 25 percent increase in the dollar price of SDR by 2015.

Sources: IMF, *International Financial Statistics* and *World Economic Outlook* (various years).

The last line in the table provides a projection of what these three ratios would look like in 10 years if there were no increase in IMF quotas (except an assumed 25 percent boost to their dollar value in connection with depreciation of the US dollar against the SDR) and with the use of compound growth rates for the period 1990–2005. Quotas would continue to decline substantially relative to foreign exchange reserves and decline relative to international trade compared with the range during the past 30

Fund declined from 58 percent of trade in 1945, to 15 percent in 1965 before the great inflation and the collapse of the Bretton Woods system, to an estimated 4 percent "at present," presumably 2003. (The last figure is higher than that shown in table 6.1, possibly because we included trade in both goods and services.) Kelkar, Chaudhry, and Vanduzer-Snow (2005) compare the size of the Fund (total IMF quotas) in 1978 at the time of the 7th quota review with the size in 1998 at the time of the 11th review. They find that the size of the Fund declined from 8.7 to 3.7 percent relative to current payments, from 1.4 to 0.9 percent relative to GDP, from 33 to 18.4 percent relative to international reserves, and from 9 to 6 percent in terms of imports. It is reasonable that quotas declined more relative to current payments than relative to imports because nontrade current account items have increased in importance over this period, but I cannot explain the large decline in the Kelkar estimates of the size of the Fund relative to imports or relative to GDP compared with the data in table 6.1.

years. For GDP, the ratio drops to the low recorded in 1990. With GDP on a PPP basis, the ratio falls 20 percent below its equivalent 1990 value.

Those who want the IMF to discharge its current responsibilities more effectively—for example, lending larger amounts in connection with capital account crises—tend to favor a substantial increase in IMF quotas in connection with the 13th quota review (Buira 2005a; Kelkar, Chaudhry, and Vanduzer-Snow 2005; Ortiz 2005). Those who envision enlarged responsibilities for the IMF tend to think the IMF will require a substantial increase in IMF resources to discharge them (Ubide 2005; Rajan 2005b). The Japanese finance minister, Sadakazu Tanigaki (2005), has expressed support for a quota increase, and his Korean colleague, Minister of Finance Hun-Jai Lee (2004), did so in stronger terms.

On the other hand, US Secretary of the Treasury Snow has stated that the United States sees no need to increase IMF quotas at this time in part because it is desirable to limit the growth in the size of the Fund in order to discourage large-scale IMF lending. Former US treasury secretary Paul O'Neill (2002) told the IMFC in September 2002, as the 12th quota review was coming to conclusion: "Limiting official resources is a key tool for increasing discipline over lending decisions." (To date, O'Neill's successor has not distanced US policy from this position.) In fact, during the past five years, the amount of IMF credit outstanding to emerging-market members of the IMF has increased by more than 20 percent. Regardless of this record and the reasons for it, using an obscure budget constraint to enforce selectivity in IMF lending is questionable international public policy compared with a need-based approach in which selectivity is based on circumstances, policy conditions, and protections.

Augmenting the IMF's Resources

During the IMF's 60 years, increases in IMF quotas have occurred on average every 6.6 years—since 1959, the average rate has been every 5.6 years.[7] However, the gap between the last two quota increases was 8 years and the previous gap was 7 years. Formal agreement on the last quota increase was reached in January 1998. Any way one looks at the historical data, they point to pressure for another increase in the next two or three years, at least by the end of the 13th quota review period in January 2008. However, don't bet on an agreement to increase IMF quotas unless policies of the major IMF members or economic and financial circumstances change dramatically from what they are today.

A more reasonable bet is that strong pressures will build for a further increase in IMF quotas by 10 years from now. One reason for action sooner rather than later is that it is difficult to imagine the IMF success-

---

7. The total of IMF quotas may increase slowly over time with the admission of new members and ad hoc adjustments in quotas, which have been rare. The text refers to increases in IMF quotas associated with general reviews of the size of the Fund.

fully addressing the issue of the distribution of IMF quotas in any context except an overall increase in quotas because each country has an individual veto over any reduction in the absolute size of its quota. In this context, the US position favoring a redistribution of quota shares but not favoring an increase in the total of IMF quotas at this time, and implicitly at any future time, is at best naive and at worst cynical. Nevertheless, as noted in chapter 4, it may be a strategic calculation.

Augmentation of standing borrowing arrangements has been even more difficult to negotiate than quota increases. Only two such augmentations have occurred since 1962 when the GAB was first established—the augmentation of the GAB in 1983 and the grafting onto the GAB of the NAB in 1998. If the IMF wants to increase its resources, it could explore two other options: borrowing from the market and gold sales.

The advantage of IMF market borrowing is that doing so requires only a simple (weighted) majority of the IMF Executive Board, not an 85 percent majority in connection with a generalized increase in quotas following a quota review. An increase in IMF quotas, in turn, must be approved by governments, starting with the US Congress. Adam Lerrick (1999) estimated that the IMF might be able to borrow in the market as much as $100 billion over time. The total that could be borrowed would be constrained by the liquid resources of the IMF and the value of its gold stock.

Bird (2003) sees IMF borrowing in the private market as a temporary countercyclical source of additional financing for the IMF. When markets are holding back in lending to developing countries, the IMF could borrow and use the resources to increase lending to those countries. He also sees such an activity as having the benefit of making the IMF more market sensitive. For Bird it is an advantage that a program of market borrowing would loosen political influences over the scale of IMF lending. Kelkar, Chaudhry, and Vanduzer-Snow (2005) make many of the same arguments. From another perspective, one disadvantage of this mechanism for augmenting IMF financial resources, other than the fact that it cannot be expanded without limit, is that it would for a substantial period remove a political constraint on IMF lending activities. Both perspectives fail to recognize that the IMF is inherently a political institution because governments own and direct it.

The approach of using the proceeds of IMF gold sales to augment IMF resources looks more attractive to some observers. IMF gold holdings are worth about $45 billion at the August 2005 market price. The IMF carries its existing gold holdings of 103.4 million ounces at about $9 billion.[8]

---

8. Before 1999, the entire IMF gold stock was valued at SDR 35 per ounce, or about $5.2 billion at the end-July 2005 dollar price of the SDR. In 1999 and 2000, the IMF increased the average value of its gold stock via transactions with Brazil and Mexico that had the effect of raising the valuation of a portion of the stock to the prevailing market price. The interest earnings on the realized capital gains from the gold transactions are being used to finance the first round of HIPC debt relief in the IMF. The capital gains will be used to support the second round.

Therefore, if the IMF could sell its gold stock at approximately the market price in August 2005 of $430 per ounce, it would realize approximately $36 billion in extra resources.[9]

In addition to providing financial resources to the IMF, sales of IMF gold holdings would help to further phase gold out of the international monetary system. Sales would provide the IMF with a significant amount of assets that could earn returns and help to finance the nonlending activities of the IMF.[10] For this reason, representatives of developing countries, for example the G-24 (2005) and Indonesian Central Bank governor, Burhanuddin Abdullah (2005), have expressed some interest in the idea along with the creation of an IMF investment account that would also generate financial returns to help support the IMF's activities.[11] However, the amount of additional resources that the IMF could raise through gold sales is not large. Moreover, some argue that IMF gold sales would weaken the IMF financially, especially if the proceeds were used to expand IMF lending. Of more practical relevance, the United States has a double veto

---

9. Some argue that the IMF sale of as much as 100 million ounces of gold on the market would severely depress the market price and cause economic damage to gold holders and produces. Dale Henderson et al. (2005) provide a theoretical argument and empirical estimates that demonstrate that this need not be the case. Their analysis is based on the assumption and revealed evidence that there is a service use of gold (for example, jewelry) as well as depletion uses (tooth fillings). They also argue that the net welfare gain associated with government gold sales now compared with delaying those sales indefinitely is substantial, about $340 billion. The net loss if the sales were delayed 20 years is estimated at $105 billion. Philipp Hildebrand (2005) offers practical evidence about how an announced program of gold sales by the Swiss National Bank over a multiyear period appears to have had little effect on the market price of gold.

10. The administrative cost of running the IMF in 2005 is more than $800 million. Some worry that if the amount of IMF lending declines permanently, the IMF will either have to cut back on its activities or increase the interest rates on its loans further.

11. Some argue that IMF borrowing countries pay a disproportionate share of IMF administrative expenses. Woods and Lombardi (2005) use a figure of 98 percent, estimated on the basis of the difference between the interest earnings of the IMF and the return that IMF creditors receive relative to the SDR interest rate on their lending to the IMF. The G-24 (2005) complains, moreover, that two-thirds of the IMF's budget is not directly related to lending activities. See in chapter 2 the brief discussion of the IMF's technical assistance activities that absorb about one-quarter of the Fund's internal resources. A relevant consideration as well is the fact that the IMF has been operating with a freeze on positions for several yeas. The Woods and Lombardi estimates are clearly too high because they ignore the underlying cost to creditor countries of lending to and through the IMF. Adam Lerrick (2003) places that figure at about $600 million for the United States alone, about seven times the figure of about $80 million Woods and Lombardi estimate for all creditor countries. Many would argue that Lerrick's figure is too high because he uses long-term interest rates to estimate the costs of US borrowing and US "loans" to the IMF are liquid claims that should be compared with short-term government borrowing rates, but the Woods and Lombardi figure is too low. Lerrick also triples his estimate to account for his assessment of the risk associated with IMF loans despite the fact that actual defaults on IMF loans have been minimal and losses can be covered by accumulated reserves.

over IMF gold sales; sales of gold require an 85 percent majority vote, and before the US treasury secretary can authorize a positive vote he must obtain the consent of the US Congress.[12]

A final proposal for financing the IMF would involve the creation of an International Financial Stability Facility (IFSF)[13] that would be financed by annual fees on stocks of cross-border investments and could be tapped by the IMF under certain circumstances to finance in whole or in part large programs of IMF financial support to systemically important countries. The IFSF is certainly not the most attractive alternative financing mechanism for the IMF, but it has the advantage of prepositioning financing from the private sector that can be disbursed, in part, for the benefit of the private sector—prepaid private-sector involvement, in other words.

The Future of SDR

Where do SDR fit into the future financing of the IMF? The IMF issues SDR to members in proportion to their quotas. SDR holdings are an alternative to foreign exchange holdings. Governments can use SDR to deal with temporary payments imbalances, just as they use foreign exchange reserves. If countries have large foreign exchange or SDR holdings, they are less likely to need to borrow from the International Monetary Fund.

The IMF issued a total of SDR 21.4 billion (about $30 billion at the dollar price of SDR at the end of July 2005) in 1970–72 and 1979–81. Under the Fourth Amendment of the IMF Articles of Agreement, an additional SDR 21.9 billion would be issued principally to those countries that joined the IMF after one or both of the issues of SDR. The IMF's Board of Governors approved the amendment in 1997. Enough members have ratified the amendment to cause it to go into force as soon as the US Congress does so. IMFC communiqués (2005) routinely call for completing the ratification of the amendment.[14]

Bird (2003, chapter 14) argues that the SDR as an alternative reserve asset in the international monetary system are destined to return to obscurity. His is an argument based on politics as well as economics. He makes this argument in a paper that was first published in 1998 following a debacle at the IMF annual meeting in Madrid on the SDR issue. At that

---

12. Neither veto is relevant to the potential "use" of gold to help "finance" the G-8 proposal for 100 percent debt relief for certain HIPC borrowers. However, the IMF self-financing of that proposal has raised a number of other issues for the IMF.

13. I made this suggestion in a speech entitled "Perspectives on International Financial Crises," to the Money Marketeers of New York University, on December 10, 2001.

14. Managing Director de Rato (IMF 2005f) reported in April 2005 that 131 members of the Fund (71 percent) with 77 percent of the votes had ratified the amendment. US ratification would raise the second figure to 94 percent.

meeting, there was a strong initial presumption promoted by Managing Director Camdessus that a positive decision would be taken to resume allocations of SDR, but the proposal was killed by the G-7 countries, which had failed to communicate clearly to Camdessus and to the rest of the IMF membership their position; alternatively, one could say Camdessus and the non-G-7 members of the Executive Board failed to understand the G-7 position before they broke for the meeting in Madrid.

The basic argument against a resumption of regular allocations of SDR is that the international monetary and financial systems have undergone profound changes since the mechanism was established in 1969, as indeed they have. The argument made is that with floating exchange rates countries do not need international reserves, or if they need reserves they can borrow them on international capital markets. The problem is that the facts do not fit the argument. Most countries do not borrow their foreign exchange reserves; they accumulate them by running current account surpluses that distort global current account positions as they force poor countries to lend to rich countries. Between 1994 and 2004 the foreign exchange reserves of emerging-market and other developing countries more than quadrupled from SDR 293 million to SDR 1,247 million.[15] Recall that the data presented in table 6.1 demonstrate a secular decline in the ratio of IMF quotas to foreign exchange reserves.

At the analytical level, Michael Mussa (1996) made the case for the allocation of SDR under the current IMF Articles of Agreement, which require a finding of "long-term global need, as and when it arises, to supplement existing reserve assets in such a manner as to promote the attainment of its [the Fund's] purposes and will avoid economic stagnation and deflation as well as excess demand and inflation in the world" (Article XVIII, 1(a)). The counterargument is that, in today's international monetary system, one can never find such a "long-term global need."

Peter Clark and Jacques Polak (2004) provided a fresh examination of this issue. They argued that a resumption of regular allocations of SDR would benefit the functioning of the international monetary system by lowering the interest cost of holding reserves and enhancing the strength of the system as a whole through greater reliance on owned versus borrowed reserves. Boyer and Truman (2005) reach a similar conclusion and stress, as well, the contribution of a resumption of SDR allocations to global cooperation and the resolution of global imbalances by lowering incentives for some countries to have essentially fixed, undervalued exchange rates. At the policy level, the Zedillo Report (UN 2002b) called for

---

15. These figures exclude the reserves of industrial countries and PRGF-eligible countries. The categories of countries are the same as those underlying tables 2.1 to 2.5. The increase for other developing countries as a group, 284 percent, was almost as large as the increase for emerging-market countries as a group, 334 percent.

the resumption of regular SDR allocations. Ariel Buira (2005a) and Stephany Griffith-Jones and Jose Antonio Ocampo (2004) do as well.

It is noteworthy that despite the opposition to the resumption of allocations of SDR, which is based on the specious argument that doing so would damage the international financial system, for example, by weakening balance of payments discipline (what discipline?) or contributing to inflation, no one to my knowledge has called for cancellation of the existing outstanding stock of SDR. Nevertheless, betting people are unlikely to place much money on the resumption of SDR allocations in connection with the original purpose of augmenting countries' holdings of international reserves.

On the other hand, a number of people advocate the modification of the purpose of SDR allocations. For example, a proposal broadly consistent with the original purpose has been made by a Council on Foreign Relations task force (1999) that advocated special allocations of SDR to fund on a one-time basis a "contingency facility" in the IMF. Richard Cooper (2002) goes further and would allow the IMF to make temporary issues of SDR to deal with financial crises and forestall creditor panics. Camdessus (Camdessus, de Larosière, and Köhler 2004) also favors selective emergency, self-liquidating SDR allocations, as do Kelkar, Chaudhry, and Vanduzer-Snow (2005) and Kelkar et al. (2005).

Departing further from the original purposes of the SDR, the G-24 (2004) continues to advocate the creation of SDR and the voluntary redistribution of them to developing countries to increase aid flows. George Soros (2002) argues for the creation of SDR to fund grants for specific global public goods and poverty reduction programs.

The best guess is that nothing will happen with respect to the SDR in the next decade or so. The Fourth Amendment will not be ratified, which is untidy; SDR will not be allocated or cancelled; and none of the proposals for stretching or transforming the role of the SDR will come to fruition. The issue of SDR is not as central to the reform of the IMF as some of the other issues that I have reviewed.

References

Abdullah, Burhanuddin. 2005. Statement on Behalf of the Southeast Asian Constituency. International Monetary and Financial Committee (April 16). Washington: International Monetary Fund.

Babb, Sarah, and Ariel Buira. 2005. Mission Creep, Mission Push and Discretion: The Case of IMF Conditionality. In *The IMF and the World Bank at Sixty*, ed. Ariel Buira. London: Anthem Press.

Barro, Robert, and Jong-Wha Lee. 2002. *IMF Programs: Who Is Chosen and What Are the Effects?* NBER Working Paper 8951. Cambridge, MA: National Bureau of Economic Research.

Bedford, Paul, Adrian Penalver, and Chris Salmon. 2005. Resolving Sovereign Debt Crises: The Market-Based Approach and the Role of the IMF. *Financial Stability Review* (Bank of England) 18 (June): 99–108.

Bevan, David. 2005. The IMF and Low-Income Countries. *World Economics* 6, no. 2 (April–June): 66–85.

Bini Smaghi, Lorenzo. 2004. A Single EU Seat in the IMF? *Journal of Common Market Studies* 42, no. 2 (June): 229–48.

Bird, Graham R. 2003. *The IMF and the Future: Issues and Options Facing the Fund*. London: Routledge.

Bird, Graham R., and D. Rowlands. 2001. IMF Lending: How Is It Influenced by Economic, Political, and Institutional Factors? *Journal of Policy Reform* 4, no. 3 (September): 243–70.

Birdsall, Nancy, and John Williamson. 2002. *Delivering on Debt Relief: From IMF Gold to a New Aid Architecture*. Washington: Center for Global Development and Institute for International Economics.

BIS (Bank for International Settlements). 2005. *75th Annual Report*. Basel: Bank for International Settlements.

Bordo, Michael D., and Harold James. 2000. *The International Monetary Fund: Its Present Role in Historical Perspective*. NBER Working Paper 7724. Prepared for the US Congressional International Financial Institution Advisory [Meltzer] Commission. Cambridge, MA: National Bureau of Economic Research.

Borensztein, Eduardo. 2004. Forces Shaping the IMF of Tomorrow. *Finance and Development* 41, no. 3 (September): 16–17.

Boughton, James M. 2001. *Silent Revolution: The International Monetary Fund, 1979–89*. Washington: International Monetary Fund.

Boughton, James M. 2004. IMF at Sixty. *Finance and Development* 41, no. 3 (September): 9–13.

Boughton, James M. 2005. Does the World Need a Universal Financial Institution? *World Economics* 6, no. 2 (April–June): 27–46.

Boyer, Jan, and Edwin M. Truman. 2005. The United States and the Large Emerging-Market Economies: Competitors or Partners? In *The United States and the World Economy: Foreign Economic Policy for the Next Decade*, ed. C. Fred Bergsten and the Institute for International Economics. Washington: Institute for International Economics.

Bradford, Colin I., and Johannes F. Linn. 2004. *Global Economic Governance at a Crossroads: Replacing the G-7 with the G-20*. Brookings Institution Policy Brief 131. Washington: Brookings Institution.

Brown, Gordon. 2005. Statement on Behalf of the United Kingdom. International Monetary and Financial Committee (April 16). Washington: International Monetary Fund.

Breton, Thierry. 2005. Statement on Behalf of France. International Monetary and Financial Committee (April 16). Washington: International Monetary Fund.

Bretton Woods Commission. 1994. *Bretton Woods: Looking to the Future*. Washington: Bretton Woods Committee.

Bryant, Ralph C. 2003. *Turbulent Waters: Cross-Border Finance and International Governance*. Washington: Brookings Institution.

Bryant, Ralph C. 2004. *Crisis Prevention and Prosperity Management for the World Economy: Policy Choices for International Governance I*. Washington: Brookings Institution.

Buira, Ariel. 2003. An Analysis of IMF Conditionality. In *Challenges to the World Bank and IMF: Developing Country Perspectives*, ed. Ariel Buira. London: Anthem Press.

Buira, Ariel. 2005a. The IMF at Sixty: An Unfulfilled Potential. In *The IMF and the World Bank at Sixty*, ed. Ariel Buira. London: Anthem Press.

Buira, Ariel. 2005b. *Reforming the Governance of the IMF and World Bank*. London: Anthem Press.

Calomiris, Charles W. 2005. International Financial Stability: What Contributions from National Policies and International Institutions. Comments prepared for a joint IMF-Bundesbank symposium, IMF in a Changing World, Frankfurt (June 8).

Calvo, Guillermo. 1998. Capital Flows and Capital-Market Crises: The Simple Economics of Sudden Stops. *Journal of Applied Economics* 1, no. 1 (May): 35–54.

Camdessus, Michel. 2005. *International Financial Institutions: Dealing with New Global Challenges*. Washington: Per Jacobsson Foundation.

Camdessus, Michel, Jacques de Larosière, and Horst Köhler. 2004. How Should the IMF Be Reshaped: Three Points of View on the IMF in the 21st Century. *Finance and Development* 41, no. 3 (September): 27–29.

Centre for Global Studies. 2004. *CFGS/CIGI Report: The G-20 at Leaders' Level*. Victoria, BC: University of Victoria.

Chami, Ralph, Sunil Sharma, and Ilhyock Shim. 2004. *A Model of the IMF as a Coinsurance Arrangement*. IMF Working Paper WP/04/219. Washington: International Monetary Fund.

Christofides, Charis, Christian Mulder, and Andrew Tiffin. 2003. *The Link Between International Standards of Good Practice, Foreign Exchange Spreads, and Ratings*. IMF Working Paper WP/03/74. Washington: International Monetary Fund.

Clark, Peter B., and Jacques J. Polak. 2004. International Liquidity and the Role of the SDR in the International Monetary System. *IMF Staff Papers* 51, no. 1 (April): 49–71.

Cohen, Daniel, and Richard Portes. 2004. *Toward a Lender of First Resort*. CEPR Discussion Paper 4615. London: Centre for Economic Policy Research.

Cooper, Richard N. 2002. Chapter 11 for Countries? *Foreign Affairs* 81, no. 4 (July/August): 90–103.

Cordella, Tito, and Eduardo Levy Yeyati. 2005. *A (New) Country Insurance Facility*. IMF Working Paper WP/05/23. Washington: International Monetary Fund.

Corsetti, Giancarlo, Bernardo Guimaraes, and Nouriel Roubini. 2003. *International Lending of Last Resort and Moral Hazard: A Model of IMF's Catalytic Finance.* NBER Working Paper 10125. Cambridge, MA: National Bureau of Economic Research.

Cottarelli, Carlo. 2005. *Efficiency and Legitimacy: Trade-Offs in IMF Governance.* IMF Working Paper WP/05/107. Washington: International Monetary Fund.

Cottarelli, Carlo, and Curzio Giannini. 2002. *Bedfellows, Hostages, or Perfect Strangers? Global Capital Markets and the Catalytic Effect of IMF Crisis Lending.* IMF Working Paper WP/02/193. Washington: International Monetary Fund.

Council on Foreign Relations. 1999. *Safeguarding Prosperity in a Global Financial System—The Future International Financial Architecture.* Report of an independent task force sponsored by the Council on Foreign Relations. New York: Council on Foreign Relations.

De Gregorio, José, Barry Eichengreen, Takatoshi Ito, and Charles Wyplosz. 1999. *An Independent and Accountable IMF.* Geneva Reports on the World Economy 1. Geneva: International Center for Monetary and Banking Studies.

Derviş, Kemal, with Ceren Özer. 2005. *A Better Globalization: Legitimacy, Government, and Reform.* Washington: Center for Global Development.

ECB (European Central Bank). 2005. *Managing Financial Crises in Emerging-Market Economies: Experience with the Involvement of Private-Sector Creditors.* Drafted by an International Relations Committee Task Force. Occasional Paper Series 32. Frankfurt: European Central Bank.

Eichel, Hans. 2005. Statement on Behalf of Germany. International Monetary and Financial Committee (April 16). Washington: International Monetary Fund.

Eichengreen, Barry. 1999. *Toward a New International Financial Architecture.* Washington: Institute for International Economics.

Eichengreen, Barry. 2004. Financial Stability. Paper prepared for the International Task Force on Global Public Goods (December).

Eichengreen, Barry, and Richard Portes. 1995. *Crisis? What Crisis? Orderly Workouts for Sovereign Debtors.* London: Centre for Economic Policy Research.

Emerging Markets. 2004. 60 for 60: Is There a Need to Change the Structure of the IMF and World Bank? *Emerging Markets 60th Anniversary Special* (October 1).

Fischer, Stanley. 1998. Capital Account Liberalization and the Role of the IMF. In *Should the IMF Pursue Capital-Account Convertibility?* Stanley Fischer, Richard N. Cooper, Rudiger Dornbusch, Peter Garber, Carlos Massad, Jacques J. Polak, Dani Rodrik, and Savak S. Tarapore. *Essays in International Finance* (Princeton University) 207 (May).

Forbes, Kristin. 2005. A Shock-Absorber Facility (SAF) for the IMF. MIT-Sloan School of Management, Cambridge, MA. Photocopy (July 18).

Friedman, Milton. 2004. 60 for 60: Is There a Need to Change the Structure of the IMF and World Bank? *Emerging Markets 60th Anniversary Special* (October 1).

G-10 (Group of Ten). 1996. The Resolution of Sovereign Debt Crises: A Report to the Ministers and Governors [Rey Report]. Basel: Bank for International Settlements.

G-24 (Intergovernmental Group of Twenty-Four on International Affairs and Development). 2004. Communiqué (October 1). Washington: International Monetary Fund.

G-24 (Intergovernmental Group of Twenty-Four on International Affairs and Development). 2005. Communiqué (April 15). Washington: International Monetary Fund.

Gelpern, Anna. 2005. *After Argentina.* International Economics Policy Brief 05-2. Washington: Institute for International Economics.

Glennerster, Rachel, and Yongseok Shin. 2003. *Is Transparency Good for You, and Can the IMF Help?* IMF Working Paper WP/03/132. Washington: International Monetary Fund.

Goldstein, Morris. 2003. An Evaluation of Proposals to Reform the International Financial Architecture. In *Managing Currency Crises in Emerging Markets,* ed. Michael P. Dooley and Jeffrey A. Frankel. Chicago: University of Chicago Press.

Goldstein, Morris. 2005a. The International Financial Architecture. In *The United States and the World Economy: Foreign Economic Policy for the Next Decade,* ed. C. Fred Bergsten and the Institute for International Economics. Washington: Institute for International Economics.

Goldstein, Morris. 2005b. *What Might the Next Emerging-Market Financial Crisis Look Like?* Working Paper 05-07. Washington: Institute for International Economics.

Goodale, Ralph. 2005. Statement on Behalf of Canada and Its IMF Constituency. International Monetary and Financial Committee (April 16). Washington: International Monetary Fund.

Griffith-Jones, Stephany, and Jose Antonio Ocampo. 2004. What Progress on International Financial Reform? Why So Limited? Document prepared for the Expert Group on Development Issues (IGDI).

Haldane, Andrew, and Mark Kruger. 2001. *The Resolution of International Financial Crises: Private Finance and Public Funds.* Bank of Canada Working Paper 2001–20. Ottawa: Bank of Canada.

Henderson, Dale W., John S. Irons, Stephen W. Salant, and Sebastian Thomas. 2005. The Benefits of Expediting Government Gold Sales. Washington: Board of Governors of the Federal Reserve System. Forthcoming in *Review of Financial Economics.*

Henning, C. Randall. 2002. *East Asian Financial Cooperation.* Washington: Institute for International Economics.

Hildebrand, Philipp M. 2005. Swiss National Bank Gold Sales: Lessons and Experience. Paper presented at the Institute for International Economics, Washington (May 5).

IFIAC (US Congressional International Financial Institutions Advisory [Meltzer] Commission). 2000. Report of the International Financial Institutions Advisory Commission. Washington: US Government Printing Office.

IMF (International Monetary Fund). 2000. Report to the IMF Executive Board of the Quota Formula Review Group (April 28). Washington.

IMF (International Monetary Fund). 2003. Access Policy in Capital Account Crises—Modifications to the Supplemental Reserve Facility (SRF) and Follow-up Issues Related to Exceptional Access (January 14). Washington.

IMF (International Monetary Fund). 2004a. From Fixed to Float: Operational Aspects of Moving Toward Exchange Rate Flexibility (November 19). Washington.

IMF (International Monetary Fund). 2004b. IMF Concludes Discussion of the Fund's Support of Low-Income Member Countries: Consideration of Instruments and Financing. Public Information Notice 04/40. Washington.

IMF (International Monetary Fund). 2004c. IMF Discusses Strengthening IMF–World Bank Collaboration on Country Programs and Conditionality—Progress Report. Public Information Notice 04/141. Washington.

IMF (International Monetary Fund). 2004d. IMF Executive Board Discusses "From Fixed to Float: Operational Aspects of Moving Toward Exchange Rate Flexibility." Public Information Notice 04/141. Washington.

IMF (International Monetary Fund). 2004e. IMF Executive Board Discusses Policy Signaling Instrument. Public Information Notice 04/114. Washington.

IMF (International Monetary Fund). 2004f. Korea—Concluding Statement of the 2004 Article IV IMF Consultation Mission (October 28). Washington.

IMF (International Monetary Fund). 2004g. Quotas—Updated Calculations (August 27). Washington.

IMF (International Monetary Fund). 2004h. Interview with Horst Köhler. *IMF Survey* 33, no. 8 (May 3): 113 and 115–16.

IMF (International Monetary Fund). 2005a. IMF Executive Board Concludes 2004 Article IV Consultation with Malaysia. Public Information Notice 05/33. Washington.

IMF (International Monetary Fund). 2005b. IMF Executive Board Has Preliminary Discussions on Charges and Maturities. Public Information Notice 05/101. Washington.

IMF (International Monetary Fund). 2005c. IMF Executive Board Reviews Experience with the Financial Sector Assessment Program. Public Information Notice 05/47. Washington.

IMF (International Monetary Fund). 2005d. IMF Executive Board Reviews the Standards and Codes Initiative. Public Information Notice 05/106. Washington.

IMF (International Monetary Fund). 2005e. People's Republic of China–Hong Kong Special Administrative Region: 2004 Article IV Consultation: Staff Report; Staff Statement; and Public Information Notice on the Executive Board Discussion. Washington.

IMF (International Monetary Fund). 2005f. Report of the Managing Director to the International Monetary and Financial Committee on the IMF's Policy Agenda (April 14). Washington.

IMF (International Monetary Fund). 2005g. Report of the Managing Director to the International Monetary and Financial Committee on the IMF's Policy Agenda (September 22). Washington.

IMF (International Monetary Fund). 2005h. Report to the International Monetary and Financial Committee on Crisis Resolution (April 12). Washington.

IMF (International Monetary Fund). 2005i. Review of the 2002 Conditionality Guidelines (March 3). Washington.

IMF (International Monetary Fund). 2005j. IMF Must Adapt to Meet Strategic Challenges. *IMF Survey* 34, no. 7 (April 25): 105.

IMF (International Monetary Fund). 2005k. The Managing Director's Report on the Fund's Medium-Term Strategy (September 15). Washington.

IMF (International Monetary Fund). 2005l. The Report of the Review Group on the Organization of Financial Sector and Capital Markets Work at the Fund (McDonough Group). Washington.

IMF (International Monetary Fund). 2005m. *World Economic Outlook* (September). Washington.

IMFC (International Monetary and Financial Committee). 2001. Draft Joint Report of the Bank Working Group for Selection of the President and the Fund Working Group to Review the Process for Selection of the Managing Director (April 29). Washington: International Monetary Fund.

IMFC (International Monetary and Financial Committee). 2005. Communiqué of the International Financial Committee of the Board of Governors of the International Monetary Fund (April 16). Washington: International Monetary Fund.

IMF-IEO (International Monetary Fund—Independent Evaluation Office). 2005a. Evaluation of the IMF's Approach to Capital Account Liberalization (April 20). Washington: International Monetary Fund.

IMF-IEO (International Monetary Fund—Independent Evaluation Office). 2005b. Evaluation of the Technical Assistance Provided by the International Monetary Fund (January 31). Washington: International Monetary Fund.

IMF-IEO (International Monetary Fund—Independent Evaluation Office). 2005c. Proposed Work Program for Fiscal Year 2006. Washington: International Monetary Fund (June 24).

IMF-IEO (International Monetary Fund—Independent Evaluation Office). 2005d. The IMF's Multilateral Surveillance: Draft Issues Paper (June 14). Washington: International Monetary Fund.

Interim Committee. 1997. Communiqué of the Interim Committee of the Board of Governors of the International Monetary Fund, Hong Kong, September 21, 1997. Washington: International Monetary Fund.

Jeanne, Olivier, and Charles Wyplosz. 2001. *The International Lender of Last Resort: How Large is Large Enough?* NBER Working Paper 8381. Cambridge, MA: National Bureau of Economic Research.

Jeanne, Olivier, and Jeromin Zettelmeyer. 2002. *"Original Sin," Balance Sheet Crises and the Roles of International Lending.* IMF Working Paper WP/02/234. Washington: International Monetary Fund.

Jeanne, Olivier, and Jeromin Zettelmeyer. 2004. *The Mussa Theorem and Other Results on IMF-Induced Moral Hazard.* IMF Working Paper WP/04/192. Washington: International Monetary Fund.

Junker, Jean-Claude. 2005. Statement on Behalf of the EU Council of Economic and Financial Ministers. International Monetary and Financial Committee (April 16). Washington: International Monetary Fund.

Kahler, Miles. 2001. *Leadership Selection in the Major Multinationals.* Washington: Institute for International Economics.

Kelkar, Vijay L., Praveen K. Chaudhry, and Marta Vanduzer-Snow. 2005. A Time for Change at the IMF: How the Institution Should Be Transformed to Address New Forces Shaping the Global Economy. *Finance and Development* 42, no. 1 (March): 46–49.

Kelkar, Vijay L., Praveen K. Chaudhry, Marta Vanduzer-Snow, and V. Bhaskar. 2005. Reforming the International Monetary Fund: Towards Enhanced Accountability and Legitimacy. In *Reforming the Governance of the IMF and the World Bank,* ed. Ariel Buira. London: Anthem Press.

Kelkar, Vijay L., Vikash Yadev, and Praveen K. Chaudhry. 2004. Reforming the Governance of the International Monetary Fund. *The World Economy* 27, no. 5 (May): 727–43.

Kenen, Peter B., Jeffrey R. Shafer, Nigel Wicks, and Charles Wyplosz. 2004. *International Economic and Financial Cooperation: New Issues, New Actors, New Responses.* Geneva Reports on the World Economy 6. Geneva: International Center for Monetary and Banking Studies.

Lane, Timothy. 2005. Tension in the Role of the IMF and Directions for Reform. *World Economics* 6, no. 2 (April–June): 47–66.

Lee, Hun-Jai. 2004. Governor for Korea and Its Constituency. Joint Annual Discussion (October 3). Washington: International Monetary Fund.

Lerrick, Adam. 1999. *Private Sector Financing for the IMF: Now Part of an Optimum Currency Mix.* Washington: Bretton Woods Committee.

Lerrick, Adam. 2003. Funding the IMF: How Much Does It Really Cost? *Quarterly International Economics Report* (Pittsburgh, Carnegie Mellon Gailliot Center for Public Policy) (November).

Lynch, Kevin G. 2005. Statement to the Senate Standing Committee on Foreign Affairs on the International Monetary Fund, Ottawa (June 7).

Martin, Paul. 2005. A Global Answer to Global Problems: The Case for a New Leaders' Forum. *Foreign Affairs* 84, no. 3 (May/June): 3–6.

Mathieu, Géraldine, Dirk Ooms, and Stéphane Rottier. 2003. The Governance of the International Monetary Fund with a Single EU Chair. *Financial Stability Review* (Brussels, National Bank of Belgium) (June): 173–88.

Meltzer, Allan H. 2005. New Mandates for the IMF and World Bank. *Cato Journal* 25, no. 1 (Winter): 13–16.

Messner, Dirk, Simon Maxwell, Franz Nuscheler, and Joseph Siegle. 2005. *Governance Reform of the Bretton Woods Institutions and the UN Development System.* Occasional Papers 17. Washington: Washington Office of the Friedrich Ebert Foundation.

Mody, Ashoka, and Diego Saravia. 2003. *Catalyzing Capital Flows: Do IMF-Supported Programs Work as Commitment Devices?* IMF Working Paper WP/03/100. Washington: International Monetary Fund.

Morris, Stephen, and Hyun Song Shin. 2003. *Catalytic Finance: When Does It Work?* Cowles Foundation Discussion Paper 1400. New Haven, CT: Cowles Foundation.

Mussa, Michael. 1996. Is There a Case for Allocation under the Present Articles? In *The Future of the SDR in Light of Changes in the International Financial System,* ed. Michael Mussa, James M. Boughton, and Peter Isard. Washington: International Monetary Fund.

O'Neill, Paul H. 2002. Statement on Behalf of the United States of America. International Monetary and Financial Committee (September 28). Washington: International Monetary Fund.

Ortiz, Guillermo. 2005. The IMF—Panacea for Every Illness? Comments prepared for a joint IMF-Bundesbank symposium, IMF in a Changing World, Frankfurt (June 8).

Peretz, David. 2005. Assessment of IMF as a Principal Institution for Promoting the Global Public Good of Financial Stability. Paper prepared for the International Task Force on Global Public Goods (January 31).

Quarles, Randal K. 2005. Statement before the Senate Banking Committee Subcommittee on International Affairs on IMF Reform (June 7).

Rajan, Raghuram. 2005a. International Financial Stability: What Contributions from National Policies and International Institutions? Comments prepared for a joint IMF-Bundesbank symposium, IMF in a Changing World, Frankfurt (June 8).

Rajan, Raghuram. 2005b. Rules versus Discretion: Should the IMF Have Less of a Free Hand in Resolving Crises? *Finance and Development* 42, no. 1 (March): 56–57.

Roubini, Nouriel, and Brad Setser. 2004. *Bailouts or Bail-Ins: Responding to Financial Crises in Emerging Economies.* Washington: Institute for International Economics.

Rubin, Robert E., and Jacob Weisberg. 2003. *In an Uncertain World: Tough Choices from Wall Street to Washington.* New York: Random House.

Siebert, Horst. 2005. Does the International Monetary System Function Efficiently? Comments prepared for a joint IMF-Bundesbank symposium, IMF in a Changing World, Frankfurt (June 8).

Siegman, Charles. 1994. The Bank for International Settlements and the Federal Reserve. *Federal Reserve Bulletin* 80 (October): 900–906.

Siniscalco, Domenico. 2005. Statement on Behalf of Italy and Its IMF Constituency. International Monetary and Financial Committee (April 16). Washington: International Monetary Fund.

Snow, John W. 2004. Statement on Behalf of the United States of America. International Monetary and Financial Committee (April 24). Washington: International Monetary Fund.

Snow, John W. 2005. Statement on Behalf of the United States of America. International Monetary and Financial Committee (April 16). Washington: International Monetary Fund.

Soros, George. 2002. *On Globalization.* New York: Public Affairs.

Tanigaki, Sadakazu. 2005. Statement on Behalf of Japan. International Monetary and Financial Committee (April 16). Washington: International Monetary Fund.

Tarullo, Daniel K. 2005. The Role of the IMF in Sovereign Debt Restructuring. *Chicago Journal of International Law* 6 (Summer): 289–311.

Truman, Edwin M. 2001. Perspectives on External Financial Crises. Speech to the Money Marketeers of New York University, December 10. Available at the Institute for International Economics web site at www.iie.com (accessed on December 20, 2005).

Truman, Edwin M. 2005a. The Euro and Prospects for Policy Coordination. In *The Euro at Five: Ready for a Global Role?* ed. Adam S. Posen. Washington: Institute for International Economics.

Truman, Edwin M. 2005b. *Postponing Global Adjustment: An Analysis of the Pending Adjustment of Global Imbalances.* Working Paper 05-6. Washington: Institute for International Economics.

Ubide, Angel. 2005. Is the IMF Business Model Still Valid? Background paper for conference, International Economic Cooperation for a Balanced World Economy, Chongqing, China. Photocopy (March 12–13).

UN (United Nations). 2002a. Report of the International Conference on Financing for Development (Monterrey Consensus) (April 18–22). New York: United Nations.

UN (United Nations). 2002b. Report of the Secretary-General's High-Level Panel on Financing Development (Zedillo Report). New York: United Nations.

UN (United Nations). 2004. Report of the Secretary-General's High-Level Panel on Threats, Challenges, and Change (December). New York: United Nations.

Van Houtven, Leo. 2002. *Governance of the IMF: Decision Making, Institutional Oversight, Transparency, and Accountability.* IMF Pamphlet 53. Washington: International Monetary Fund.

Van Houtven, Leo. 2004. Rethinking IMF Governance. *Finance and Development* 41, no. 3 (September): 18–20.

Williamson, John. 1985. *The Exchange Rate System.* POLICY ANALYSES IN INTERNATIONAL ECONOMICS 5. Washington: Institute for International Economics.

Williamson, John. 2000. *Exchange Rate Regimes for Emerging Markets: Reviving the Intermediate Option.* POLICY ANALYSES IN INTERNATIONAL ECONOMICS 60. Washington: Institute for International Economics.

Williamson, John. 2001. The Role of the IMF: A Guide to the Reports. In *Developing Countries and the Global Financial System,* ed. Stephany Griffith-Jones and Amar Bhattacharya. London: The Commonwealth Secretariat.

Williamson, John. 2005. *Curbing the Boom-Bust Cycle: Stabilizing Capital Flows to Emerging Markets.* POLICY ANALYSES IN INTERNATIONAL ECONOMICS 75. Washington: Institute for International Economics.

Woods, Ngaire, and Domenico Lombardi. 2005. *Effective Representation and the Role of Coalitions within the IMF.* Working Paper. Oxford: Global Economic Governance Program.

Zeti, Akhtar Aziz. 2004. The IMF and World Bank: Key Challenges. Roundtable in *Emerging Markets 60th Anniversary Special* (October 1).

Index

accountability. *See* transparency
Adams, Timothy, 3–4
Argentina, 36, 55, 88–89, 94, 95–97
ASEAN+3, 70
Asian Bond Fund, 58
Asian monetary fund, 38–39, 57–58

Bank for International Settlements (BIS), 38, 57, 57*n*
Brady Plan, 97, 97*n*
Brazil, 79, 87
Breton, Thierry, 77*n*, 100, 105
Bretton Woods
  Agreements Act, 61*n*
  Commission, 39–40, 57*n*, 65*n*
  Committee, 47, 96, 100
  conference (1944), 31*n*, 47*n*, 57*n*, 65*n*
  institutions (BWI), 8*b*, 12, 25–27, 63, 80

Camdessus, Michel, 50, 57–58, 95, 114–15
  reform agenda, 6, 7*b*–8*b*
Canada, 10
Chiang Mai Initiative, 38, 58
China, 10, 79
collective action clauses (CACs), 42, 93–94
Committee of Twenty (C-20), 78
Compensatory Financing Facility (CFF), 29, 83
"conditionality," 83*n*

contingent credit lines (CCLs), 84, 99
Council of EU Finance Ministers, 76
Country Policy and Institutional
  Assessment (CPIA) system, 17, 17*n*

Denmark, 10
de Rato, Rodrigo, 2–6, 16–18, 20, 23, 72, 91
  Argentine crisis and, 96
  exchange rates and, 51
  IMFC and, 56
  Report on the Fund's Medium-Term
    Strategy, 2*b*–3*b*
developing countries, 10, 32*t*–36*t*
Development Committee, 12, 63

Ecuador, 87
emerging-market countries, 2*n*, 7*b*–8*b*,
  9–12, 14, 32*t*–33*t*, 93
  classification, 31, 31*n*
  economic crises and, 42–43, 64
  foreign exchange reserves, 37–39, 114,
    114*n*
  outstanding credit, 4–5, 33, 34–40,
    34*t*–36*t*, 89, 110
  preconditions, loan, 99
  reform issues and, 47–49
  shares and chairs and, 8*b*, 73–77
  stability and growth of, 97–98
  support for, nonfinancial, 101–102

European Union, 79
  IMF Executive Board and, 9, 20n–21n,
    75–77
  quotas and voting shares, 10–12, 11n,
    67, 67n, 69, 71
exceptional access, 89, 91–93
Extended Fund Facility (EFF), 29, 83

Financial Sector Assessment Program
  (FSAP), 28n, 53

Geithner, Timothy, 47–48, 96, 100
gold, 103, 107, 111–13, 111n, 112n
governance, 5–6, 7b–8b, 20, 26, 47–50, 58
  (see also Medium-Term Strategy)
  Executive Board, chairs, 73–77
  management and staff, 71–73
  quotas and voting shares, 3b, 5–6, 8b,
    9–12, 19–21, 38–41, 62, 64–71, 108–10
  steering committees, 77–81
Group of Five (G-5), 78n
Group of Seven (G-7), 5, 5n, 12, 27, 62, 78,
  78n, 102
Group of Eight (G-8), 8b
Group of Ten (G-10), 5, 5n, 62, 78, 78n
Group of Eleven (G-11), 62
Group of Twenty (G-20), 5, 5n, 11, 12, 62,
  79–80
Group of Twenty-Four (G-24), 5, 5n

Heavily Indebted Poor Countries (HIPC)
  program, 35, 103–105, 103n, 111n, 113n
Hong Kong, 52

illiquidity and insolvency, 88–89, 90
IMFC. See International Monetary and
  Financial Committee (IMFC)
Independent Evaluation Office (IEO),
  48–49, 53, 54n, 55
India, 79
Indonesia, 15, 50, 62n–63n, 89, 98
industrial countries, 5n, 13n, 31–38,
  32t–33t, 38n
  outstanding credit, 34t–36t
Interim Committee, 54
International Financial Institutions
  Advisory Commission (IFIAC 2000),
  41, 99, 105
International Monetary and Financial
  Committee (IMFC), 2b–3b, 4–5, 8b, 12,
  43–44
  exchange rates and, 51–52
International Monetary Fund (IMF)
  administrative expenses, 111, 111n

Articles of Agreement, 8b, 17–18, 20, 23,
  26, 27
Bank for International Settlements (BIS)
  and, 38, 57, 57n
borrowers, 84–87, 85t
Brady Plan, 97
capital accounts and financial sector,
  4–5, 17–18, 24, 52–56, 54n
"code of conduct," 93, 93n
contingent credit lines (CCL), 84, 99
core activities, 25, 27
debt restructuring, 7b, 14–15, 90–99,
  103–105 (see also Heavily Indebted
  Poor Countries (HIPC) program)
developing countries, 10, 32t–36t
emerging-market countries, 2n, 7b–8b,
  9–12, 14, 32t–33t, 93: classification, 31,
  31n; economic crises and, 42–43, 64;
  foreign exchange reserves, 37–39, 114,
  114n; outstanding credit, 4–5, 33,
  34–40, 34t–36t, 89, 110; preconditions,
  loan, 99; reform issues and, 47–49;
  shares and chairs and, 8b, 73–77;
  stability and growth of, 97–98;
  support for, nonfinancial, 101–102
financial stability and, 14–15, 24–26,
  29n, 40–43, 49–53, 62–64, 87–90, 89n,
  99
Fourth Amendment to Articles, 56, 107
global imbalances, 5–6, 12, 46–53, 52n,
  66–67, 79, 83, 114
governance of, 5–6, 7b–8b, 20, 26, 47–50,
  58 (see also Medium-Term Strategy):
  executive board, chairs, 73–77;
  management and staff, 71–73; quotas
  and voting shares, 3b, 5–6, 8b, 9–12,
  19–21, 38–41, 62, 64–71, 108–10;
  steering committees, 77–81
industrial countries, 5n, 13n, 31–38,
  32t–33t, 38n: outstanding credit,
  34t–36t
insurance facility, 99–100
lending, 34t–36t: arrangements and
  facilities, 31–39, 83–106, 83n;
  contingent credit lines (CCLs), 84, 99;
  exceptional access, 43, 89–93; "good
  performers" and, 98–100;
  indebtedness and, 97–98
low-income countries, 1–6, 16–17, 20,
  30, 41–43, 63–64, 90, 101–106
Medium-Term Strategy, 2–4, 2b–3b
mission, 7b–8b, 23–28, 46, 62
organizations, relations with, 56–57

PRGF-eligible countries, 32t–33t, 84,
114n: outstanding credit, 30–38, 30n,
34t–36t; support for, 102–6
quotas and voting shares, 3b, 5–6, 8b,
9–12, 19–21, 39–41, 62, 64–71, 108–10
reform, 1–2, 2b–3b, 7b–8b (see also
reform issues): case for, 2–4;
components, 4–6, 40–44, 47–50
regional development banks, 57–58
reviews and consultations (Article IV),
13, 24, 28, 37n, 39n, 49, 97–98, 100,
106: Hong Kong, 52; Korea, 52
special drawing rights (SDR), 6, 21n, 59,
109, 113–15
support, nonfinancial, 100–102
surveillance, 2b, 4, 6, 7b, 46–52: capital
accounts and financial sectors, 52–56;
exchange rates, 50–52
systemically important countries, 1–2,
2n, 6, 12–14, 13n, 20, 48–50, 53, 61–62,
79n, 113
tools, 28–30
World Bank and, 16–17, 18, 27, 57, 63
World Trade Organization (WTO) and,
57
Ireland, 9, 10

Japan, 10, 53

Köhler, Horst, 72, 76, 91–92
Korea, 10, 52, 62n–63n

Larosière, Jacques de, 50, 92, 95–96
lending, 34t–36t
arrangements and facilities, 31–39,
83–106, 83n
contingent credit lines (CCLs), 84, 99
exceptional access, 43, 89–93
"good performers" and, 98–100
indebtedness and, 97–98
low-income countries, 1–6, 16–17, 20, 30,
41–43, 63–64, 90, 101–106
Luxembourg, 10

Malaysia, 10
McDonough Group, 18, 27
Meltzer, Allan, 25, 105
Meltzer Commission, 41, 99, 105
Mexico, 10, 62n–63n, 79, 87
Millennium Development Goals, 2b
Monterrey Consensus, 63
moral hazard, 91

Organization for Economic Cooperation
and Development (OECD), 57

Poland, 9
Policy Support Instrument, 17
Poverty Reduction and Growth Facility
(PRGF), 17, 29–30, 83
Poverty Reduction Strategy Papers
(PRSP), 17, 30
PRGF-eligible countries, 32t–33t, 84, 114n
outstanding credit, 30–38, 30n, 34t–36t
support for, 102–106

Quarles, Randal, 27, 42, 70–71, 102
quotas and voting shares, 3b, 5–6, 8b,
9–12, 19–21, 39–41, 62, 64–71, 108–10

real resources, transfer of, 7b–8b, 8n
reform issues, 7b–8b, 47–50, 58
capital accounts and financial sector,
4–5, 17–18, 24, 52–56, 54n
debt restructuring, 7b, 90–99, 103–105
(see also Heavily Indebted Poor
Countries (HIPC) program)
Fourth Amendment to Articles, 56, 107
"good performers," 98–100
governance. See under International
Monetary Fund (IMF), governance
indebted countries, support for, 97–98
lending. See under International
Monetary Fund (IMF), lending
low-income members, engagement
with, 16–17, 102–10
macroeconomic and exchange rate
policies, 12–14
management, 12, 71–73
mission, 7b–8b, 23–24, 23–28, 46, 62
necessity of, 2–6
nonfinancial support, 100–102
previous efforts, 39–44
quotas and voting shares, 3b, 5–6, 8b,
9–12, 19–21, 38–41, 62, 64–71,
108–10
regional development banks, 57–58
requisites, 1–2
SDR allocations, 113–15
shares and chairs, 8b, 10–11, 73–77
steering committees, 77–81
surveillance. See under International
Monetary Fund (IMF), surveillance
time criticality, 20
regional development banks, 57–58

Report of the Secretary-General's High-Level Panel on Threats, Challenges, and Change, 80
Report on the Fund's Medium-Term Strategy (de Rato), 2b–3b
Reports on Observance of Standards and Codes (ROSCs), 27, 28n, 29, 37n, 39n, 53, 53n
Review Group on the Organization of Financial Sector and Capital Markets Work. See McDonough Group
Russia, 87

SDR. See special drawing rights (SDR)
Singapore, 10
Smithsonian Agreement, 78
Snow, John, 21n, 23, 42, 70, 102, 104
South Africa, 79
Soviet Union, 26
Spain, 9, 10
Special Data Dissemination Standard (SDDS), 59
special drawing rights (SDR), 6, 21n, 59, 109, 113–15
Stability and Growth Facility (SGF), 97–98
Stand-By Arrangements (SBA), 29, 80
Summers, Lawrence, 41–42, 78
Supplemental Reserve Facility (SRF), 29, 83

surveillance, 2b, 4, 6, 7b, 46–52
capital accounts and financial sectors, 52–56
exchange rates, 50–52
systemically important countries, 1–2, 2n, 6, 12–14, 13n, 20, 48–50, 53, 61–62, 79n, 113

Tanigaki, Sadakazu, 70
Thailand, 10, 62n–63n, 87
transparency, 26, 27n, 41–42, 47–48, 61, 74, 93
Turkey, 10, 15, 89, 92

United States, 9, 10–11, 53, 64, 68, 68n, 79
Uruguay, 15, 36, 89, 94, 98

Volcker, Paul, 50
voting shares. See quotas and voting shares

Wolfensohn, James, 72
Wolfowitz, Paul, 16, 72
World Bank, 18, 27, 57, 72, 103–106
Country Policy and Institutional Assessment (CPIA) system, 17, 17n
World Trade Organization (WTO), 57, 72

Zedillo Report, 114–15

Other Publications from the Institute for International Economics

WORKING PAPERS

94-1 APEC and Regional Trading Arrangements in the Pacific
Jeffrey A. Frankel with Sang-Jin Wei and Ernesto Stein

94-2 Towards an Asia Pacific Investment Code Edward M. Graham

94-3 Merchandise Trade in the APEC Region: Is There Scope for Liberalization on an MFN Basis? Paul Wonnacott

94-4 The Automotive Industry in Southeast Asia: Can Protection Be Made Less Costly? Paul Wonnacott

94-5 Implications of Asian Economic Growth Marcus Noland

95-1 APEC: The Bogor Declaration and the Path Ahead C. Fred Bergsten

95-2 From Bogor to Miami . . . and Beyond: Regionalism in the Asia Pacific and the Western Hemisphere Jeffrey J. Schott

95-3 Has Asian Export Performance Been Unique? Marcus Noland

95-4 Association of Southeast Asian Nations (ASEAN) and ASEAN Free Trade Area (AFTA): Chronology and Statistics Gautam Jaggi

95-5 The North Korean Economy Marcus Noland

95-6 China and the International Economic System Marcus Noland

96-1 APEC after Osaka: Toward Free Trade by 2010/2020 C. Fred Bergsten

96-2 Public Policy, Private Preferences, and the Japanese Trade Pattern Marcus Noland

96-3 German Lessons for Korea: The Economics of Unification Marcus Noland

96-4 Research and Development Activities and Trade Specialization in Japan Marcus Noland

96-5 China's Economic Reforms: Chronology and Statistics Gautam Jaggi, Mary Rundle, Daniel Rosen, and Yuichi Takahashi

96-6 US-China Economic Relations Marcus Noland

96-7 The Market Structure Benefits of Trade and Investment Liberalization Raymond Atje and Gary Hufbauer

96-8 The Future of US-Korea Economic Relations Marcus Noland

96-9 Competition Policies in the Dynamic Industrializing Economies: The Case of China, Korea, and Chinese Taipei Edward M. Graham

96-10 Modeling Economic Reform in North Korea Marcus Noland, Sherman Robinson, and Monica Scatasta

96-11 Trade, Investment, and Economic Conflict Between the United States and Asia Marcus Noland

96-12 APEC in 1996 and Beyond: The Subic Summit C. Fred Bergsten

96-13 Some Unpleasant Arithmetic Concerning Unification Marcus Noland

96-14 Restructuring Korea's Financial Sector for Greater Competitiveness Marcus Noland

96-15 Competitive Liberalization and Global Free Trade: A Vision for the 21st Century C. Fred Bergsten

97-1 Chasing Phantoms: The Political Economy of USTR Marcus Noland

97-2 US-Japan Civil Aviation: Prospects for Progress Jacqueline McFadyen

97-3 Open Regionalism C. Fred Bergsten

97-4 Lessons from the Bundesbank on the Occasion of Its 40th (and Second to Last?) Birthday Adam S. Posen

97-5 The Economics of Korean Unification Marcus Noland, Sherman Robinson, and Li-Gang Liu

98-1 The Costs and Benefits of Korean Unification Marcus Noland, Sherman Robinson, and Li-Gang Liu

98-2 Asian Competitive Devaluations Li-Gang Liu, Marcus Noland, Sherman Robinson, and Zhi Wang

98-3 Fifty Years of the GATT/WTO: Lessons from the Past for Strategies for the Future C. Fred Bergsten

98-4 NAFTA Supplemental Agreements: Four Year Review Jacqueline McFadyen

98-5 Local Government Spending: Solving the Mystery of Japanese Fiscal Packages Hiroko Ishii and Erika Wada

98-6 The Global Economic Effects of the Japanese Crisis Marcus Noland, Sherman Robinson, and Zhi Wang

99-1   Rigorous Speculation: The Collapse and Revival of the North Korean Economy   Marcus Noland, Sherman Robinson, and Tao Wang

99-2   Famine in North Korea: Causes and Cures   Marcus Noland, Sherman Robinson, and Tao Wang

99-3   Competition Policy and FDI: A Solution in Search of a Problem?   Marcus Noland

99-4   The Continuing Asian Financial Crisis: Global Adjustment and Trade   Marcus Noland, Sherman Robinson, and Zhi Wang

99-5   Why EMU Is Irrelevant for the German Economy   Adam S. Posen

99-6   The Global Trading System and the Developing Countries in 2000   C. Fred Bergsten

99-7   Modeling Korean Unification   Marcus Noland, Sherman Robinson, and Tao Wang

99-8   Sovereign Liquidity Crisis: The Strategic Case for a Payments Standstill   Marcus Miller and Lei Zhang

99-9   The Case for Joint Management of Exchange Rate Flexibility   C. Fred Bergsten, Olivier Davanne, and Pierre Jacquet

99-10   Does Talk Matter After All? Inflation Targeting and Central Bank Behavior   Kenneth N. Kuttner and Adam S. Posen

99-11   Hazards and Precautions: Tales of International Finance   Gary Clyde Hufbauer and Erika Wada

99-12   The Globalization of Services: What Has Happened? What Are the Implications?   Gary C. Hufbauer and Tony Warren

00-1   Regulatory Standards in the WTO: Comparing Intellectual Property Rights with Competition Policy, Environmental Protection, and Core Labor Standards   Keith Maskus

00-2   International Economic Agreements and the Constitution   Richard M. Goodman and John M. Frost

00-3   Electronic Commerce in Developing Countries: Issues for Domestic Policy and WTO Negotiations   Catherine L. Mann

00-4   The New Asian Challenge   C. Fred Bergsten

00-5   How the Sick Man Avoided Pneumonia: The Philippines in the Asian Financial Crisis   Marcus Noland

00-6   Inflation, Monetary Transparency, and G-3 Exchange Rate Volatility   Kenneth N. Kuttner and Adam S. Posen

00-7   Transatlantic Issues in Electronic Commerce   Catherine L. Mann

00-8   Strengthening the International Financial Architecture: Where Do We Stand?   Morris Goldstein

00-9   On Currency Crises and Contagion   Marcel Fratzscher

01-1   Price Level Convergence and Inflation in Europe   John H. Rogers, Gary Clyde Hufbauer, and Erika Wada

01-2   Subsidies, Market Closure, Cross-Border Investment, and Effects on Competition: The Case of FDI in the Telecommunications Sector   Edward M. Graham

01-3   Foreign Direct Investment in China: Effects on Growth and Economic Performance   Edward M. Graham and Erika Wada

01-4   IMF Structural Conditionality: How Much Is Too Much?   Morris Goldstein

01-5   Unchanging Innovation and Changing Economic Performance in Japan   Adam S. Posen

01-6   Rating Banks in Emerging Markets: What Credit Rating Agencies Should Learn from Financial Indicators   Liliana Rojas-Suarez

01-7   Beyond Bipolar: A Three-Dimensional Assessment of Monetary Frameworks   Kenneth N. Kuttner and Adam S. Posen

01-8   Finance and Changing US-Japan Relations: Convergence Without Leverage—Until Now   Adam S. Posen

01-9   Macroeconomic Implications of the New Economy   Martin Neil Baily

01-10   Can International Capital Standards Strengthen Banks in Emerging Markets?   Liliana Rojas-Suarez

02-1   Moral Hazard and the US Stock Market: Analyzing the "Greenspan Put"?   Marcus Miller, Paul Weller, and Lei Zhang

02-2   Passive Savers and Fiscal Policy Effectiveness in Japan   Kenneth N. Kuttner and Adam S. Posen

02-3   Home Bias, Transaction Costs, and Prospects for the Euro: A More Detailed Analysis   Catherine L. Mann and Ellen E. Meade

02-4   Toward a Sustainable FTAA: Does Latin America Meet the Necessary Financial Preconditions?   Liliana Rojas-Suarez

02-5   Assessing Globalization's Critics: "Talkers Are No Good Doers???"   Kimberly Ann Elliott, Debayani Kar, and J. David Richardson

02-6   Economic Issues Raised by
Treatment of Takings under NAFTA
Chapter 11   Edward M. Graham

03-1   Debt Sustainability, Brazil, and
the IMF   Morris Goldstein

03-2   Is Germany Turning Japanese?
Adam S. Posen

03-3   Survival of the Best Fit: Exposure
to Low-Wage Countries and the
(Uneven) Growth of US
Manufacturing Plants
Andrew B. Bernard, J. Bradford
Jensen, and Peter K. Schott

03-4   Falling Trade Costs,
Heterogeneous Firms, and
Industry Dynamics
Andrew B. Bernard, J. Bradford
Jensen, and Peter K. Schott

03-5   Famine and Reform in North Korea
Marcus Noland

03-6   Empirical Investigations in
Inflation Targeting   Yifan Hu

03-7   Labor Standards and the Free
Trade Area of the Americas
Kimberly Ann Elliott

03-8   Religion, Culture, and Economic
Performance   Marcus Noland

03-9   It Takes More than a Bubble to
Become Japan   Adam S. Posen

03-10   The Difficulty of Discerning
What's Too Tight: Taylor Rules
and Japanese Monetary Policy
Adam S. Posen/Kenneth N. Kuttner

04-1   Adjusting China's Exchange Rate
Policies   Morris Goldstein

04-2   Popular Attitudes, Globalization,
and Risk   Marcus Noland

04-3   Selective Intervention and Growth:
The Case of Korea   Marcus Noland

05-1   Outsourcing and Offshoring:
Pushing the European Model Over
the Hill, Rather Than Off the Cliff!
Jacob Funk Kirkegaard

05-2   China's Role in the Revived
Bretton Woods System:
A Case of Mistaken Identity
Morris Goldstein and
Nicholas Lardy

05-3   Affinity and International Trade
Marcus Noland

05-4   South Korea's Experience with International
Capital Flows   Marcus Noland

05-5   Explaining Middle Eastern
Authoritarianism   Marcus Noland

05-6   Postponing Global Adjustment:
An Analysis of the Pending Adjustment
of Global Imbalances   Edwin Truman

05-7   What Might the Next Emerging-
Market Financial Crisis Look Like?
Morris Goldstein, assisted by Anna
Wong

05-8   Egypt after the Multi-Fiber
Arrangement
Dan Magder

05-9   Tradable Services: Understanding
the Scope and Impact of Services
Offshoring   J. Bradford Jensen
and Lori G. Kletzer

05-10   Importers, Exporters, and Multina-
tionals: A Portrait of Firms in the
U.S. that Trade Goods
Andrew B. Bernard, J. Bradford
Jensen, and Peter K. Schott

05-11   The US Trade Deficit: A Disaggre-
gated Perspective   Catherine
L. Mann and Katharina Plück

05-12   Prospects for Regional Free Trade
in Asia   Gary Clyde Hufbauer
and Yee Wong

05-13   Predicting Trade Expansion under
FTAs and Multilateral Agreements
Dean A. DeRosa and John P. Gilbert

05-14   The East Asian Industrial Policy
Experience: Implications for the
Middle East
Marcus Noland and Howard Pack

05-15   Outsourcing and Skill Imports:
Foreign High-Skilled Workers on
H-1B and L-1 Visas in the United
States   Jacob Funk Kirkegaard

POLICY BRIEFS

98-1   The Asian Financial Crisis
Morris Goldstein

98-2   The New Agenda with China
C. Fred Bergsten

98-3   Exchange Rates for the Dollar,
Yen, and Euro   Simon Wren-Lewis

98-4   Sanctions-Happy USA
Gary Clyde Hufbauer

98-5   The Depressing News from Asia
Marcus Noland, Sherman
Robinson, and Zhi Wang

98-6   The Transatlantic Economic
Partnership   Ellen L. Frost

98-7   A New Strategy for the Global
Crisis   C. Fred Bergsten

98-8   Reviving the "Asian Monetary
Fund"   C. Fred Bergsten

99-1   Implementing Japanese Recovery
Adam S. Posen

99-2   A Radical but Workable
         Restructuring Plan for South Korea
         Edward M. Graham
99-3   Crawling Bands or Monitoring
         Bands: How to Manage Exchange
         Rates in a World of Capital
         Mobility   John Williamson
99-4   Market Mechanisms to Reduce the
         Need for IMF Bailouts
         Catherine L. Mann
99-5   Steel Quotas: A Rigged Lottery
         Gary C. Hufbauer and Erika Wada
99-6   China and the World Trade
         Organization: An Economic
         Balance Sheet   Daniel H. Rosen
99-7   Trade and Income Distribution:
         The Debate and New Evidence
         William R. Cline
99-8   Preserve the Exchange Stabilization
         Fund   C. Randall Henning
99-9   Nothing to Fear but Fear (of
         Inflation) Itself   Adam S. Posen
99-10   World Trade after Seattle:
         Implications for the United States
         Gary Clyde Hufbauer
00-1   The Next Trade Policy Battle
         C. Fred Bergsten
00-2   Decision-making in the WTO
         Jeffrey J. Schott and Jayashree Watal
00-3   American Access to China's Market:
         The Congressional Vote on PNTR
         Gary C. Hufbauer and Daniel Rosen
00-4   Third Oil Shock: Real or Imaginary?
         Consequences and Policy
         Alternatives   Philip K. Verleger Jr.
00-5   The Role of the IMF: A Guide to
         the Reports   John Williamson
00-6   The ILO and Enforcement of Core
         Labor Standards   Kimberly Ann Elliott
00-7   "No" to Foreign Telecoms Equals
         "No" to the New Economy!
         Gary C. Hufbauer/Edward M. Graham
01-1   Brunei: A Turning Point for APEC?
         C. Fred Bergsten
01-2   A Prescription to Relieve Worker
         Anxiety   Lori Kletzer/Robert E. Litan
01-3   The US Export-Import Bank: Time for
         an Overhaul   Gary C. Hufbauer
01-4   Japan 2001 — Decisive Action or
         Financial Panic   Adam S. Posen
01-5   Fin(d)ing Our Way on Trade and
         Labor Standards?
         Kimberly Ann Elliott
01-6   Prospects for Transatlantic
         Competition Policy   Mario Monti

01-7   The International Implications of
         Paying Down the Debt
         Edwin M. Truman
01-8   Dealing with Labor and Environment
         Issues in Trade Promotion
         Legislation   Kimberly Ann Elliott
01-9   Steel: Big Problems, Better Solutions
         Gary Clyde Hufbauer/Ben Goodrich
01-10   Economic Policy Following the
         Terrorist Attacks   Martin Neil Baily
01-11   Using Sanctions to Fight Terrorism
         Gary Clyde Hufbauer, Jeffrey J. Schott,
         and Barbara Oegg
02-1   Time for a Grand Bargain in Steel?
         Gary C. Hufbauer and Ben Goodrich
02-2   Prospects for the World Economy:
         From Global Recession to Global
         Recovery   Michael Mussa
02-3   Sovereign Debt Restructuring:
         New Articles, New Contracts — or
         No Change?   Marcus Miller
02-4   Support the Ex-Im Bank: It Has
         Work to Do!   Gary Clyde Hufbauer
         and Ben Goodrich
02-5   The Looming Japanese Crisis
         Adam S. Posen
02-6   Capital-Market Access: New
         Frontier in the Sanctions Debate
         Gary C. Hufbauer and Barbara Oegg
02-7   Is Brazil Next?   John Williamson
02-8   Further Financial Services
         Liberalization in the Doha Round?
         Wendy Dobson
02-9   Global Economic Prospects
         Michael Mussa
02-10   The Foreign Sales Corporation:
         Reaching the Last Act?
         Gary Clyde Hufbauer
03-1   Steel Policy: The Good, the Bad,
         and the Ugly   Gary Clyde Hufbauer
         and Ben Goodrich
03-2   Global Economic Prospects:
         Through the Fog of Uncertainty
         Michael Mussa
03-3   Economic Leverage and the North
         Korean Nuclear Crisis
         Kimberly Ann Elliott-
03-4   The Impact of Economic Sanctions
         on US Trade: Andrew Rose's
         Gravity Model   Gary Clyde
         Hufbauer and Barbara Oegg
03-5   Reforming OPIC for the 21st Century
         Theodore H. Moran/C. Fred Bergsten
03-6   The Strategic Importance of
         US-Korea Economic Relations
         Marcus Noland

03-7 Rules Against Earnings Stripping:
Wrong Answer to Corporate
Inversions
Gary Clyde Hufbauer and Ariel Assa
03-8 More Pain, More Gain: Politics
and Economics of Eliminating Tariffs
Gary C. Hufbauer and Ben Goodrich
03-9 EU Accession and the Euro: Close
Together or Far Apart?
Peter B. Kenen and Ellen E. Meade
03-10 Next Move in Steel: Revocation or
Retaliation? Gary Clyde Hufbauer
and Ben Goodrich
03-11 Globalization of IT Services and
White Collar Jobs: The Next Wave
of Productivity Growth
Catherine L. Mann
04-1 This Far and No Farther? Nudging
Agricultural Reform Forward
Tim Josling and Dale Hathaway
04-2 Labor Standards, Development,
and CAFTA Kimberly Ann Elliott
04-3 Senator Kerry on Corporate Tax
Reform: Right Diagnosis, Wrong
Prescription Gary Clyde Hufbauer
and Paul Grieco
04-4 Islam, Globalization, and Economic
Performance in the Middle East
Marcus Noland and Howard Pack
04-5 China Bashing 2004
Gary Clyde Hufbauer and Yee Wong
04-6 What Went Right in Japan
Adam S. Posen
04-7 What Kind of Landing for the
Chinese Economy? Morris Goldstein
and Nicholas R. Lardy
05-1 A Currency Basket for East Asia,
Not Just China John Williamson
05-2 After Argentina
Anna Gelpern
05-3 Living with Global Imbalances:
A Contrarian View
Richard N. Cooper
05-4 The Case for a New Plaza Agreement
William R. Cline
06-1 The United States Needs German
Economic Leadership
Adam S. Posen

* = out of print

POLICY ANALYSES IN
INTERNATIONAL ECONOMICS Series

1 The Lending Policies of the International
Monetary Fund* John Williamson
August 1982 ISBN 0-88132-000-5
2 "Reciprocity": A New Approach to World
Trade Policy?* William R. Cline
September 1982 ISBN 0-88132-001-3
3 Trade Policy in the 1980s*
C. Fred Bergsten and William R. Cline
November 1982 ISBN 0-88132-002-1
4 International Debt and the Stability of the
World Economy* William R. Cline
September 1983 ISBN 0-88132-010-2
5 The Exchange Rate System,* Second Edition
John Williamson
Sept. 1983, rev. June 1985 ISBN 0-88132-034-X
6 Economic Sanctions in Support of Foreign
Policy Goals*
Gary Clyde Hufbauer and Jeffrey J. Schott
October 1983 ISBN 0-88132-014-5
7 A New SDR Allocation?* John Williamson
March 1984 ISBN 0-88132-028-5
8 An International Standard for Monetary
Stabilization* Ronald L. McKinnon
March 1984 ISBN 0-88132-018-8
9 The Yen/Dollar Agreement: Liberalizing
Japanese Capital Markets* Jeffrey A. Frankel
December 1984 ISBN 0-88132-035-8
10 Bank Lending to Developing Countries: The
Policy Alternatives* C. Fred Bergsten,
William R. Cline, and John Williamson
April 1985 ISBN 0-88132-032-3
11 Trading for Growth: The Next Round of
Trade Negotiations*
Gary Clyde Hufbauer and Jeffrey J. Schott
September 1985 ISBN 0-88132-033-1
12 Financial Intermediation Beyond the Debt
Crisis* Donald R. Lessard, John Williamson
September 1985 ISBN 0-88132-021-8
13 The United States-Japan Economic Problem*
C. Fred Bergsten and William R. Cline
October 1985, 2d ed. January 1987
ISBN 0-88132-060-9
14 Deficits and the Dollar: The World Economy
at Risk* Stephen Marris
December 1985, 2d ed. November 1987
ISBN 0-88132-067-6
15 Trade Policy for Troubled Industries*
Gary Clyde Hufbauer and Howard R. Rosen
March 1986 ISBN 0-88132-020-X

16 The United States and Canada: The Quest for Free Trade* Paul Wonnacott, with an appendix by John Williamson
March 1987 ISBN 0-88132-056-0

17 Adjusting to Success: Balance of Payments Policy in the East Asian NICs*
Bela Balassa and John Williamson
June 1987, rev. April 1990 ISBN 0-88132-101-X

18 Mobilizing Bank Lending to Debtor Countries* William R. Cline
June 1987 ISBN 0-88132-062-5

19 Auction Quotas and United States Trade Policy* C. Fred Bergsten, Kimberly Ann Elliott, Jeffrey J. Schott, and Wendy E. Takacs
September 1987 ISBN 0-88132-050-1

20 Agriculture and the GATT: Rewriting the Rules* Dale E. Hathaway
September 1987 ISBN 0-88132-052-8

21 Anti-Protection: Changing Forces in United States Trade Politics*
I. M. Destler and John S. Odell
September 1987 ISBN 0-88132-043-9

22 Targets and Indicators: A Blueprint for the International Coordination of Economic Policy
John Williamson and Marcus H. Miller
September 1987 ISBN 0-88132-051-X

23 Capital Flight: The Problem and Policy Responses* Donald R. Lessard and John Williamson
December 1987 ISBN 0-88132-059-5

24 United States-Canada Free Trade: An Evaluation of the Agreement*
Jeffrey J. Schott
April 1988 ISBN 0-88132-072-2

25 Voluntary Approaches to Debt Relief*
John Williamson
Sept.1988, rev. May 1989 ISBN 0-88132-098-6

26 American Trade Adjustment: The Global Impact* William R. Cline
March 1989 ISBN 0-88132-095-1

27 More Free Trade Areas?*
Jeffrey J. Schott
May 1989 ISBN 0-88132-085-4

28 The Progress of Policy Reform in Latin America* John Williamson
January 1990 ISBN 0-88132-100-1

29 The Global Trade Negotiations: What Can Be Achieved?* Jeffrey J. Schott
September 1990 ISBN 0-88132-137-0

30 Economic Policy Coordination: Requiem or Prologue?* Wendy Dobson
April 1991 ISBN 0-88132-102-8

31 The Economic Opening of Eastern Europe*
John Williamson
May 1991 ISBN 0-88132-186-9

32 Eastern Europe and the Soviet Union in the World Economy*
Susan M. Collins and Dani Rodrik
May 1991 ISBN 0-88132-157-5

33 African Economic Reform: The External Dimension* Carol Lancaster
June 1991 ISBN 0-88132-096-X

34 Has the Adjustment Process Worked?*
Paul R. Krugman
October 1991 ISBN 0-88132-116-8

35 From Soviet disUnion to Eastern Economic Community?*
Oleh Havrylyshyn and John Williamson
October 1991 ISBN 0-88132-192-3

36 Global Warming: The Economic Stakes*
William R. Cline
May 1992 ISBN 0-88132-172-9

37 Trade and Payments After Soviet Disintegration* John Williamson
June 1992 ISBN 0-88132-173-7

38 Trade and Migration: NAFTA and Agriculture* Philip L. Martin
October 1993 ISBN 0-88132-201-6

39 The Exchange Rate System and the IMF: A Modest Agenda Morris Goldstein
June 1995 ISBN 0-88132-219-9

40 What Role for Currency Boards?
John Williamson
September 1995 ISBN 0-88132-222-9

41 Predicting External Imbalances for the United States and Japan* William R. Cline
September 1995 ISBN 0-88132-220-2

42 Standards and APEC: An Action Agenda*
John S. Wilson
October 1995 ISBN 0-88132-223-7

43 Fundamental Tax Reform and Border Tax Adjustments* Gary Clyde Hufbauer
January 1996 ISBN 0-88132-225-3

44 Global Telecom Talks: A Trillion Dollar Deal*
Ben A. Petrazzini
June 1996 ISBN 0-88132-230-X

45 WTO 2000: Setting the Course for World Trade Jeffrey J. Schott
September 1996 ISBN 0-88132-234-2

46 The National Economic Council: A Work in Progress * I. M. Destler
November 1996 ISBN 0-88132-239-3

47 The Case for an International Banking Standard Morris Goldstein
April 1997 ISBN 0-88132-244-X

48 Transatlantic Trade: A Strategic Agenda*
Ellen L. Frost
May 1997 ISBN 0-88132-228-8

49 **Cooperating with Europe's Monetary Union**
C. Randall Henning
May 1997   ISBN 0-88132-245-8

50 **Renewing Fast Track Legislation*** I. M. Destler
September 1997   ISBN 0-88132-252-0

51 **Competition Policies for the Global Economy**
Edward M. Graham and J. David Richardson
November 1997   ISBN 0-88132-249-0

52 **Improving Trade Policy Reviews in the World
Trade Organization**   Donald Keesing
April 1998   ISBN 0-88132-251-2

53 **Agricultural Trade Policy: Completing the
Reform**   Timothy Josling
April 1998   ISBN 0-88132-256-3

54 **Real Exchange Rates for the Year 2000**
Simon Wren Lewis and Rebecca Driver
April 1998   ISBN 0-88132-253-9

55 **The Asian Financial Crisis: Causes, Cures,
and Systemic Implications** Morris Goldstein
June 1998   ISBN 0-88132-261-X

56 **Global Economic Effects of the Asian
Currency Devaluations**
Marcus Noland, LiGang Liu, Sherman
Robinson, and Zhi Wang
July 1998   ISBN 0-88132-260-1

57 **The Exchange Stabilization Fund: Slush
Money or War Chest?** C. Randall Henning
May 1999   ISBN 0-88132-271-7

58 **The New Politics of American Trade: Trade,
Labor, and the Environment**
I. M. Destler and Peter J. Balint
October 1999   ISBN 0-88132-269-5

59 **Congressional Trade Votes: From NAFTA
Approval to Fast Track Defeat**
Robert E. Baldwin and Christopher S. Magee
February 2000   ISBN 0-88132-267-9

60 **Exchange Rate Regimes for Emerging
Markets: Reviving the Intermediate Option**
John Williamson
September 2000   ISBN 0-88132-293-8

61 **NAFTA and the Environment: Seven Years
Later**   Gary Clyde Hufbauer, Daniel
Esty, Diana Orejas, Luis Rubio, and
Jeffrey J. Schott
October 2000   ISBN 0-88132-299-7

62 **Free Trade between Korea and the United
States?** Inbom Choi and Jeffrey J. Schott
April 2001   ISBN 0-88132-311-X

63 **New Regional Trading Arrangements in the
Asia Pacific?**
Robert Scollay and John P. Gilbert
May 2001   ISBN 0-88132-302-0

64 **Parental Supervision: The New Paradigm
for Foreign Direct Investment and
Development**   Theodore H. Moran
August 2001   ISBN 0-88132-313-6

65 **The Benefits of Price Convergence:
Speculative Calculations**
Gary Clyde Hufbauer, Erika Wada,
and Tony Warren
December 2001   ISBN 0-88132-333-0

66 **Managed Floating Plus**
Morris Goldstein
March 2002   ISBN 0-88132-336-5

67 **Argentina and the Fund: From Triumph
to Tragedy**   Michael Mussa
July 2002   ISBN 0-88132-339-X

68 **East Asian Financial Cooperation**
C. Randall Henning
September 2002   ISBN 0-88132-338-1

69 **Reforming OPIC for the 21st Century**
Theodore H. Moran
May 2003   ISBN 0-88132-342-X

70 **Awakening Monster: The Alien Tort
Statute of 1789**
Gary C. Hufbauer and Nicholas Mitrokostas
July 2003   ISBN 0-88132-366-7

71 **Korea after Kim Jong-il**
Marcus Noland
January 2004   ISBN 0-88132-373-X

72 **Roots of Competitiveness: China's Evolving
Agriculture Interests**   Daniel H. Rosen,
Scott Rozelle, and Jikun Huang
July 2004   ISBN 0-88132-376-4

73 **Prospects for a US-Taiwan FTA**
Nicholas R. Lardy and Daniel H. Rosen
December 2004   ISBN 0-88132-367-5

74 **Anchoring Reform with a US-Egypt
Free Trade Agreement**
Ahmed Galal and Robert Z. Lawrence
April 2005   ISBN 0-88132-368-3

75 **Curbing the Boom-Bust Cycle: Stabilizing
Capital Flows to Emerging Markets**
John Williamson
July 2005   ISBN 0-88132-330-6

76 **The Shape of a US-Switzerland Free Trade
Agreement**
Gary Clyde Hufbauer and Richard E. Baldwin
February 2006   ISBN 978-0-88132-385-6

77 **A Strategy for IMF Reform**
Edwin M. Truman
February 2006   ISBN 978-0-88132-398-6

BOOKS

IMF Conditionality* John Williamson, editor
1983   ISBN 0-88132-006-4
Trade Policy in the 1980s* William R. Cline, ed.
1983   ISBN 0-88132-031-5
Subsidies in International Trade*
Gary Clyde Hufbauer and Joanna Shelton Erb
1984   ISBN 0-88132-004-8

International Debt: Systemic Risk and Policy
Response* William R. Cline
1984 ISBN 0-88132-015-3
Trade Protection in the United States: 31 Case
Studies* Gary Clyde Hufbauer, Diane E. Berliner,
and Kimberly Ann Elliott
1986 ISBN 0-88132-040-4
Toward Renewed Economic Growth in Latin
America* Bela Balassa, Gerardo M. Bueno, Pedro-
Pablo Kuczynski, and Mario Henrique Simonsen
1986 ISBN 0-88132-045-5
Capital Flight and Third World Debt*
Donald R. Lessard and John Williamson, editors
1987 ISBN 0-88132-053-6
The Canada-United States Free Trade Agreement:
The Global Impact*
Jeffrey J. Schott and Murray G. Smith, editors
1988 ISBN 0-88132-073-0
World Agricultural Trade: Building a Consensus*
William M. Miner and Dale E. Hathaway, editors
1988 ISBN 0-88132-071-3
Japan in the World Economy*
Bela Balassa and Marcus Noland
1988 ISBN 0-88132-041-2
America in the World Economy: A Strategy for
the 1990s* C. Fred Bergsten
1988 ISBN 0-88132-089-7
Managing the Dollar: From the Plaza to the
Louvre* Yoichi Funabashi
1988, 2d. ed. 1989 ISBN 0-88132-097-8
United States External Adjustment and the World
Economy* William R. Cline
May 1989 ISBN 0-88132-048-X
Free Trade Areas and U.S. Trade Policy*
Jeffrey J. Schott, editor
May 1989 ISBN 0-88132-094-3
Dollar Politics: Exchange Rate Policymaking in
the United States*
I. M. Destler and C. Randall Henning
September 1989 ISBN 0-88132-079-X
Latin American Adjustment: How Much Has
Happened?* John Williamson, editor
April 1990 ISBN 0-88132-125-7
The Future of World Trade in Textiles and
Apparel* William R. Cline
1987, 2d ed. June 1999 ISBN 0-88132-110-9
Completing the Uruguay Round: A Results-
Oriented Approach to the GATT Trade
Negotiations* Jeffrey J. Schott, editor
September 1990 ISBN 0-88132-130-3
Economic Sanctions Reconsidered (2 volumes)
Economic Sanctions Reconsidered:
Supplemental Case Histories
Gary Clyde Hufbauer, Jeffrey J. Schott, and
Kimberly Ann Elliott
1985, 2d ed. Dec. 1990 ISBN cloth 0-88132-115-X
ISBN paper 0-88132-105-2

Economic Sanctions Reconsidered: History and
Current Policy Gary Clyde Hufbauer,
Jeffrey J. Schott, and Kimberly Ann Elliott
December 1990 ISBN cloth 0-88132-140-0
ISBN paper 0-88132-136-2
Pacific Basin Developing Countries: Prospects for
Economic Sanctions Reconsidered: History
and Current Policy Gary Clyde Hufbauer,
Jeffrey J. Schott, and Kimberly Ann Elliott
December 1990 ISBN cloth 0-88132-140-0
ISBN paper 0-88132-136-2
Pacific Basin Developing Countries: Prospects
for the Future* Marcus Noland
January 1991 ISBN cloth 0-88132-141-9
ISBN paper 0-88132-081-1
Currency Convertibility in Eastern Europe*
John Williamson, editor
October 1991 ISBN 0-88132-128-1
International Adjustment and Financing: The
Lessons of 1985-1991* C. Fred Bergsten, editor
January 1992 ISBN 0-88132-112-5
North American Free Trade: Issues and
Recommendations*
Gary Clyde Hufbauer and Jeffrey J. Schott
April 1992 ISBN 0-88132-120-6
Narrowing the U.S. Current Account Deficit*
Alan J. Lenz/June 1992 ISBN 0-88132-103-6
The Economics of Global Warming
William R. Cline/June 1992 ISBN 0-88132-132-X
US Taxation of International Income: Blueprint
for Reform* Gary Clyde Hufbauer,
assisted by Joanna M. van Rooij
October 1992 ISBN 0-88132-134-6
Who's Bashing Whom? Trade Conflict in High-
Technology Industries Laura D'Andrea Tyson
November 1992 ISBN 0-88132-106-0
Korea in the World Economy* Il SaKong
January 1993 ISBN 0-88132-183-4
Pacific Dynamism and the International
Economic System*
C. Fred Bergsten and Marcus Noland, editors
May 1993 ISBN 0-88132-196-6
Economic Consequences of Soviet Disintegration*
John Williamson, editor
May 1993 ISBN 0-88132-190-7
Reconcilable Differences? United States-Japan
Economic Conflict*
C. Fred Bergsten and Marcus Noland
June 1993 ISBN 0-88132-129-X
Does Foreign Exchange Intervention Work?
Kathryn M. Dominguez and Jeffrey A. Frankel
September 1993 ISBN 0-88132-104-4
Sizing Up U.S. Export Disincentives*
J. David Richardson
September 1993 ISBN 0-88132-107-9

NAFTA: An Assessment
Gary Clyde Hufbauer and Jeffrey J. Schott/*rev. ed.*
October 1993   ISBN 0-88132-199-0

Adjusting to Volatile Energy Prices
Philip K. Verleger, Jr.
November 1993   ISBN 0-88132-069-2

The Political Economy of Policy Reform
John Williamson, editor
January 1994   ISBN 0-88132-195-8

Measuring the Costs of Protection
in the United States
Gary Clyde Hufbauer and Kimberly Ann Elliott
January 1994   ISBN 0-88132-108-7

The Dynamics of Korean Economic Development*
Cho Soon/*March 1994*   ISBN 0-88132-162-1

Reviving the European Union*
C. Randall Henning, Eduard Hochreiter, and
Gary Clyde Hufbauer, editors
April 1994   ISBN 0-88132-208-3

China in the World Economy   Nicholas R. Lardy
April 1994   ISBN 0-88132-200-8

Greening the GATT: Trade, Environment, and
the Future   Daniel C. Esty
July 1994   ISBN 0-88132-205-9

Western Hemisphere Economic Integration*
Gary Clyde Hufbauer and Jeffrey J. Schott
July 1994   ISBN 0-88132-159-1

Currencies and Politics in the United States,
Germany, and Japan   C. Randall Henning
September 1994   ISBN 0-88132-127-3

Estimating Equilibrium Exchange Rates
John Williamson, editor
September 1994   ISBN 0-88132-076-5

Managing the World Economy: Fifty Years after
Bretton Woods   Peter B. Kenen, editor
September 1994   ISBN 0-88132-212-1

Reciprocity and Retaliation in U.S. Trade Policy
Thomas O. Bayard and Kimberly Ann Elliott
September 1994   ISBN 0-88132-084-6

The Uruguay Round: An Assessment*
Jeffrey J. Schott, assisted by Johanna W. Buurman
November 1994   ISBN 0-88132-206-7

Measuring the Costs of Protection in Japan*
Yoko Sazanami, Shujiro Urata, and Hiroki Kawai
January 1995   ISBN 0-88132-211-3

Foreign Direct Investment in the United States,
3d ed., Edward M. Graham and Paul R. Krugman
January 1995   ISBN 0-88132-204-0

The Political Economy of Korea-United States
Cooperation*
C. Fred Bergsten and Il SaKong, editors
February 1995   ISBN 0-88132-213-X

International Debt Reexamined* William R. Cline
February 1995   ISBN 0-88132-083-8

American Trade Politics, 3d ed., I. M. Destler
April 1995   ISBN 0-88132-215-6

Asia Pacific Fusion: Japan's Role in APEC*
Yoichi Funabashi
October 1995   ISBN 0-88132-224-5

Korea-United States Cooperation in the New
World Order*
C. Fred Bergsten and Il SaKong, editors
February 1996   ISBN 0-88132-226-1

Why Exports Really Matter!* ISBN 0-88132-221-0
Why Exports Matter More!* ISBN 0-88132-229-6
J. David Richardson and Karin Rindal
July 1995; February 1996

Global Corporations and National Governments
Edward M. Graham
May 1996   ISBN 0-88132-111-7

Global Economic Leadership and the Group of
Seven   C. Fred Bergsten and C. Randall Henning
May 1996   ISBN 0-88132-218-0

The Trading System after the Uruguay Round*
John Whalley and Colleen Hamilton
July 1996   ISBN 0-88132-131-1

Private Capital Flows to Emerging Markets after
the Mexican Crisis*   Guillermo A. Calvo,
Morris Goldstein, and Eduard Hochreiter
September 1996   ISBN 0-88132-232-6

The Crawling Band as an Exchange Rate Regime:
Lessons from Chile, Colombia, and Israel
John Williamson
September 1996   ISBN 0-88132-231-8

Flying High: Liberalizing Civil Aviation in the
Asia Pacific*
Gary Clyde Hufbauer and Christopher Findlay
November 1996   ISBN 0-88132-227-X

Measuring the Costs of Visible Protection
in Korea*   Namdoo Kim
November 1996   ISBN 0-88132-236-9

The World Trading System: Challenges Ahead
Jeffrey J. Schott
December 1996   ISBN 0-88132-235-0

Has Globalization Gone Too Far? Dani Rodrik
March 1997   ISBN cloth 0-88132-243-1

Korea-United States Economic Relationship*
C. Fred Bergsten and Il SaKong, editors
March 1997   ISBN 0-88132-240-7

Summitry in the Americas: A Progress Report
Richard E. Feinberg
April 1997   ISBN 0-88132-242-3

Corruption and the Global Economy
Kimberly Ann Elliott
June 1997   ISBN 0-88132-233-4

Regional Trading Blocs in the World Economic
System   Jeffrey A. Frankel
October 1997   ISBN 0-88132-202-4

Sustaining the Asia Pacific Miracle:
Environmental Protection and Economic
Integration   Andre Dua and Daniel C. Esty
October 1997   ISBN 0-88132-250-4

Trade and Income Distribution   William R. Cline
November 1997   ISBN 0-88132-216-4
Global Competition Policy
Edward M. Graham and J. David Richardson
December 1997   ISBN 0-88132-166-4
Unfinished Business: Telecommunications
after the Uruguay Round
Gary Clyde Hufbauer and Erika Wada
December 1997   ISBN 0-88132-257-1
Financial Services Liberalization in the WTO
Wendy Dobson and Pierre Jacquet
June 1998   ISBN 0-88132-254-7
Restoring Japan's Economic Growth
Adam S. Posen
September 1998   ISBN 0-88132-262-8
Measuring the Costs of Protection in China
Zhang Shuguang, Zhang Yansheng, and Wan
Zhongxin
November 1998   ISBN 0-88132-247-4
Foreign Direct Investment and Development:
The New Policy Agenda for Developing
Countries and Economies in Transition
Theodore H. Moran
December 1998   ISBN 0-88132-258-X
Behind the Open Door: Foreign Enterprises
in the Chinese Marketplace
Daniel H. Rosen
January 1999   ISBN 0-88132-263-6
Toward A New International Financial
Architecture: A Practical Post-Asia Agenda
Barry Eichengreen
February 1999   ISBN 0-88132-270-9
Is the U.S. Trade Deficit Sustainable?
Catherine L. Mann
September 1999   ISBN 0-88132-265-2
Safeguarding Prosperity in a Global Financial
System: The Future International Financial
Architecture, Independent Task Force Report
Sponsored by the Council on Foreign Relations
Morris Goldstein, Project Director
October 1999   ISBN 0-88132-287-3
Avoiding the Apocalypse: The Future of the
Two Koreas   Marcus Noland
June 2000   ISBN 0-88132-278-4
Assessing Financial Vulnerability: An Early
Warning System for Emerging Markets
Morris Goldstein, Graciela Kaminsky, and
Carmen Reinhart
June 2000   ISBN 0-88132-237-7
Global Electronic Commerce: A Policy Primer
Catherine L. Mann, Sue E. Eckert, and Sarah
Cleeland Knight
July 2000   ISBN 0-88132-274-1
The WTO after Seattle   Jeffrey J. Schott, editor
July 2000   ISBN 0-88132-290-3

Intellectual Property Rights in the Global
Economy   Keith E. Maskus
August 2000   ISBN 0-88132-282-2
The Political Economy of the Asian Financial
Crisis   Stephan Haggard
August 2000   ISBN 0-88132-283-0
Transforming Foreign Aid: United States
Assistance in the 21st Century   Carol Lancaster
August 2000   ISBN 0-88132-291-1
Fighting the Wrong Enemy: Antiglobal Activists
and Multinational Enterprises Edward M. Graham
September 2000   ISBN 0-88132-272-5
Globalization and the Perceptions of American
Workers
Kenneth F. Scheve and Matthew J. Slaughter
March 2001   ISBN 0-88132-295-4
World Capital Markets: Challenge to the G-10
Wendy Dobson and Gary Clyde Hufbauer,
assisted by Hyun Koo Cho
May 2001   ISBN 0-88132-301-2
Prospects for Free Trade in the Americas
Jeffrey J. Schott/*August 2001*   ISBN 0-88132-275-X
Toward a North American Community:
Lessons from the Old World for the New
Robert A. Pastor/*August 2001* ISBN 0-88132-328-4
Measuring the Costs of Protection in Europe:
European Commercial Policy in the 2000s
Patrick A. Messerlin
September 2001   ISBN 0-88132-273-3
Job Loss from Imports: Measuring the Costs
Lori G. Kletzer
September 2001   ISBN 0-88132-296-2
No More Bashing: Building a New Japan–United
States Economic Relationship   C. Fred Bergsten,
Takatoshi Ito, and Marcus Noland
October 2001   ISBN 0-88132-286-5
Why Global Commitment Really Matters!
Howard Lewis III and J. David Richardson
October 2001   ISBN 0-88132-298-9
Leadership Selection in the Major Multilaterals
Miles Kahler
November 2001   ISBN 0-88132-335-7
The International Financial Architecture:
What's New? What's Missing?   Peter Kenen
November 2001   ISBN 0-88132-297-0
Delivering on Debt Relief: From IMF Gold
to a New Aid Architecture
John Williamson and Nancy Birdsall,
with Brian Deese
April 2002   ISBN 0-88132-331-4
Imagine There's No Country: Poverty,
Inequality, and Growth in the Era
of Globalization   Surjit S. Bhalla
September 2002   ISBN 0-88132-348-9

Reforming Korea's Industrial Conglomerates
Edward M. Graham
January 2003   ISBN 0-88132-337-3
Industrial Policy in an Era of Globalization:
Lessons from Asia
Marcus Noland and Howard Pack
March 2003   ISBN 0-88132-350-0
Reintegrating India with the World Economy
T. N. Srinivasan and Suresh D. Tendulkar
March 2003   ISBN 0-88132-280-6
After the Washington Consensus:
Restarting Growth and Reform
in Latin America   Pedro-Pablo Kuczynski
and John Williamson, editors
March 2003   ISBN 0-88132-347-0
The Decline of US Labor Unions and
the Role of Trade   Robert E. Baldwin
June 2003   ISBN 0-88132-341-1
Can Labor Standards Improve
under Globalization?
Kimberly Ann Elliott and Richard B. Freeman
June 2003   ISBN 0-88132-332-2
Crimes and Punishments? Retaliation
under the WTO   Robert Z. Lawrence
October 2003   ISBN 0-88132-359-4
Inflation Targeting in the World Economy
Edwin M. Truman
October 2003   ISBN 0-88132-345-4
Foreign Direct Investment and Tax
Competition   John H. Mutti
November 2003   ISBN 0-88132-352-7
Has Globalization Gone Far Enough?
The Costs of Fragmented Markets
Scott Bradford and Robert Z. Lawrence
February 2004   ISBN 0-88132-349-7
Food Regulation and Trade:
Toward a Safe and Open Global System
Tim Josling, Donna Roberts, and David Orden
March 2004   ISBN 0-88132-346-2
Controlling Currency Mismatches in
Emerging Markets
Morris Goldstein and Philip Turner
April 2004   ISBN 0-88132-360-8
Free Trade Agreements: US Strategies
and Priorities   Jeffrey J. Schott, editor
April 2004   ISBN 0-88132-361-6
Trade Policy and Global Poverty
William R. Cline
June 2004   ISBN 0-88132-365-9
Bailouts or Bail-ins? Responding
to Financial Crises in Emerging Economies
Nouriel Roubini and Brad Setser
August 2004   ISBN 0-88132-371-3
Transforming the European Economy
Martin Neil Baily and Jacob Kirkegaard
September 2004   ISBN 0-88132-343-8

Chasing Dirty Money: The Fight Against
Money Laundering
Peter Reuter and Edwin M. Truman
November 2004   ISBN 0-88132-370-5
The United States and the World Economy:
Foreign Economic Policy for the Next Decade
C. Fred Bergsten
January 2005   ISBN 0-88132-380-2
Does Foreign Direct Investment Promote
Development ?   Theodore Moran, Edward
M. Graham, and Magnus Blomström, editors
April 2005   ISBN 0-88132-381-0
American Trade Politics, 4th ed.
I. M. Destler
June 2005   ISBN 0-88132-382-9
Why Does Immigration Divide America?
Public Finance and Political Opposition
to Open Borders
Gordon Hanson
August 2005   ISBN 0-88132-400-0
Reforming the US Corporate Tax
Gary Clyde Hufbauer and Paul L. E. Grieco
September 2005   ISBN 0-88132-384-5
The United States as a Debtor Nation
William R. Cline
September 2005   ISBN 0-88132-399-3
NAFTA Revisited: Achievements
and Challenges
Gary Clyde Hufbauer and Jeffrey J. Schott,
assisted by Paul L. E. Grieco and Yee Wong
October 2005   ISBN 0-88132-334-9

SPECIAL REPORTS

1   **Promoting World Recovery: A Statement**
      on Global Economic Strategy*
      by 26 Economists from Fourteen Countries
      December 1982   ISBN 0-88132-013-7
2   **Prospects for Adjustment in Argentina,**
      Brazil, and Mexico: Responding to the
      Debt Crisis*   John Williamson, editor
      June 1983   ISBN 0-88132-016-1
3   **Inflation and Indexation: Argentina, Brazil,**
      and Israel*   John Williamson, editor
      March 1985   ISBN 0-88132-037-4
4   **Global Economic Imbalances***
      C. Fred Bergsten, editor
      March 1986   ISBN 0-88132-042-0
5   **African Debt and Financing***
      Carol Lancaster and John Williamson, eds.
      May 1986   ISBN 0-88132-044-7
6   **Resolving the Global Economic Crisis:**
      After Wall Street*   by Thirty-three
      Economists from Thirteen Countries
      December 1987   ISBN 0-88132-070-6

7   World Economic Problems*
     Kimberly Ann Elliott/John Williamson, eds.
     April 1988   ISBN 0-88132-055-2
     Reforming World Agricultural Trade*
     by Twenty-nine Professionals from Seventeen
     Countries/*1988*   ISBN 0-88132-088-9
8   Economic Relations Between the United
     States and Korea: Conflict or Cooperation?*
     Thomas O. Bayard and Soogil Young, eds.
     January 1989   ISBN 0-88132-068-4
9   Whither APEC? The Progress to Date
     and Agenda for the Future*
     C. Fred Bergsten, editor
     October 1997   ISBN 0-88132-248-2
10   Economic Integration of the Korean
     Peninsula   Marcus Noland, editor
     January 1998   ISBN 0-88132-255-5
11   Restarting Fast Track* Jeffrey J. Schott, ed.
     April 1998   ISBN 0-88132-259-8
12   Launching New Global Trade Talks:
     An Action Agenda Jeffrey J. Schott, ed.
     September 1998   ISBN 0-88132-266-0
13   Japan's Financial Crisis and Its Parallels
     to US Experience
     Ryoichi Mikitani and Adam S. Posen, eds.
     September 2000   ISBN 0-88132-289-X
14   The Ex-Im Bank in the 21st Century: A New
     Approach   Gary Clyde Hufbauer
     and Rita M. Rodriguez, editors
     January 2001   ISBN 0-88132-300-4
15   The Korean Diaspora in the World Economy
     C. Fred Bergsten and Inbom Choi, eds.
     January 2003   ISBN 0-88132-358-6
16   Dollar Overvaluation and the World
     Economy
     C. Fred Bergsten and John Williamson, eds.
     February 2003   ISBN 0-88132-351-9
17   Dollar Adjustment: How Far? Against What?
     C. Fred Bergsten and John Williamson, eds.
     November 2004   ISBN 0-88132-378-0
18   The Euro at Five: Ready for a Global Role?
     Adam S. Posen, editor
     April 2005   ISBN 0-88132-380-2

WORKS IN PROGRESS

Case Studies in US Trade Negotiation,
Vols. 1 and 2
Robert Z. Lawrence, Charan Devereaux,
and Michael Watkins
Accelerating the Globalization of America:
Information Technology
Catherine L. Mann

Delivering on Doha: Farm Trade and the Poor
Kimberly Ann Elliott
Foreign Direct Investment and US National
Security
Edward M. Graham and David Marchick
Reform in a Rich Country: Germany
Adam S. Posen
Global Forces, American Faces: US Economic
Globalization at the Grass Roots
J. David Richardson
The Future of Chinese Exchange Rates
Morris Goldstein and Nicholas R. Lardy
Reforming the International Monetary Fund
for the 21st Century
Edwin M. Truman, ed.
The Arab Economies in a Changing World
Marcus Noland and Howard Pack
Economic Regionalism in East Asia
C. Fred Bergsten and C. Randall Henning
The Strategic Implications of China-Taiwan
Economic Relations
Nicholas R. Lardy
Financial Crises and the Future
of Emerging Markets
William R. Cline
US Taxation of International Income, 2d ed.
Gary Clyde Hufbauer and Ariel Assa
Prospects for a US-Colombia Free Trade
Agreement
Jeffrey J. Schott
Prospects for a Middle East Free Trade
Agreement
Robert Z. Lawrence
Prospects for a Sri Lanka Free Trade
Agreement
Dean DeRosa
Workers at Risk: Job Loss from Apparel,
Textiles, Footwear, and Furniture
Lori G. Kletzer
Economic Sanctions Reconsidered, 3rd. ed.
Kimberly Ann Elliott, Gary C. Hufbauer,
and Jeffrey J. Schott
The Impact of Global Services Outsourcing
on American Firms and Workers
J. Bradford Jensen, Lori G. Kletzer,
and Catherine L. Mann
Rethinking US Social Security:
Drawing on World Best Practices
Martin N. Baily

DISTRIBUTORS OUTSIDE THE UNITED STATES

**Australia, New Zealand,
and Papua New Guinea**
D. A. Information Services
648 Whitehorse Road
Mitcham, Victoria 3132, Australia
Tel: 61-3-9210-7777
Fax: 61-3-9210-7788
Email: service@dadirect.com.au
www.dadirect.com.au

Canada
Renouf Bookstore
5369 Canotek Road, Unit 1
Ottawa, Ontario KlJ 9J3, Canada
Tel: 613-745-2665
Fax: 613-745-7660
www.renoufbooks.com

India, Bangladesh, Nepal, and Sri Lanka
Viva Books Pvt.
Mr. Vinod Vasishtha
4325/3, Ansari Rd.
Daryaganj, New Delhi-110002
India
Tel: 91-11-327-9280
Fax: 91-11-326-7224
Email: viva@vivagroupindia.com
www.vivagroupindia.com

Japan
United Publishers Services Ltd.
1-32-5, Higashi-shinagawa
Shinagawa-ku, Tokyo 140-0002
Japan
Tel: 81-3-5479-7251
Fax: 81-3-5479-7307
Email: purchasing@ups.co.jp
*For trade accounts only. Individuals will find
IIE books in leading Tokyo bookstores.*

**Mexico, Central America, South America,
and Puerto Rico**
US PubRep, Inc.
311 Dean Drive
Rockville, MD 20851
Tel: 301-838-9276
Fax: 301-838-9278
Email: c.falk@ieee.org
www.uspubrep.com

Middle East
MERIC
2 Bahgat Ali Street, El Masry Towers
Tower D, Apt. 24
Zamalek, Cairo
Egypt
Tel. 20-2-7633824
Fax: 20-2-7369355
Email: mahmoud_fouda@mericonline.com
www.mericonline.com

Southeast Asia *(Brunei, Burma, Cambodia,
Indonesia, Malaysia, the Philippines,
Singapore, Taiwan, Thailand, and Vietnam)*
APAC Publishers Services PTE Ltd.
70 Bendemeer Road #05-03
Hiap Huat House
Singapore 333940
Tel: 65-6844-7333
Fax: 65-6747-8916
Email: service@apacmedia.com.sg

United Kingdom, Europe
(including Russia and Turkey), **Africa,
and Israel**
The Eurospan Group
c/o Turpin Distribution
Pegasus Drive
Stratton Business Park
Biggleswade, Bedfordshire
SG18 8TQ
United Kingdom
Tel: 44 (0) 1767-604972
Fax: 44 (0) 1767-601640
Email: eurospan@turpin-distribution.com
www.eurospangroup.com/bookstore

**Visit our Web site at:
www.iie.com
E-mail orders to:
IIE mail@PressWarehouse.com**